Paul and His Life-Transforming Theology

Paul
and His Life-Transforming Theology

A Concise Introduction

ROGER MOHRLANG

WIPF *&* STOCK · Eugene, Oregon

PAUL AND HIS LIFE-TRANSFORMING THEOLOGY
A Concise Introduction

Wipf & Stock
An Imprint of Wipf and Stock Publishers
199 W. 8th Ave., Suite 3
Eugene, OR 97401

www.wipfandstock.com

ISBN 13: 978-1-61097-870-5

To Dot

"Gift of God"

"Wheresoever I open St Paul's Epistles, I meet not words but thunder, and universal thunder, thunder that passes through all the world."

—J. DONNE

Contents

Preface

THIS BOOK IS DESIGNED to be a concise, inviting introduction to the greatest of the early Christian missionaries, the Apostle Paul—his life, his letters, his thinking—and the amazing Good News he was given to proclaim to the world.

Written in non-technical language for Christian students and Christian readers generally, this book should be helpful to any student of the Bible who desires a deeper understanding of Paul, his theology, and his message. My hope is that the book will express something of the fire in Paul's heart and the power of his gospel, and whet the reader's appetite for careful study of his letters themselves. (No amount of other reading can ever substitute for the study of Scripture itself.)

Let me be candid: I write as a lifelong lover of Paul's letters. These letters have transformed my life, and I shall be forever grateful for them. As a new convert to Christ, I first felt the power of these letters during my undergraduate years at Carnegie Institute of Technology (now Carnegie Mellon University). My fascination with them grew in the years that followed, when I was engaged in Bible translation in northeastern Nigeria. My understanding of them was deepened in the course of my doctoral study on Matthew and Paul at the University of Oxford. But it has been the repeated reading, study, and teaching of Paul's letters over the last thirty-plus years (most of it at Whitworth University but some of it overseas[1]) that has made them my life and my love. This small book, the result of a lifetime of studying and teaching these letters, is an expression of my appreciation for all they have meant to me.

I write as a Christian believer who takes seriously the authority of Scripture as the Word of God. But this in no way diminishes my conviction of the importance of understanding each letter in the light of its own

1. In England, Cameroon, Kenya, India, Nepal, China, and the Philippines.

historical setting—and that takes careful reading and hard work. (Paul's letters are intellectually challenging, to say the least.) Interpreters of Paul must pay scrupulous attention to the historical, social, and literary context of each passage, even as they seek to understand his theological thinking as a whole. If they fail to read carefully, they run the risk of misunderstanding him. Christian believers, then, must learn to read these letters both prayerfully and analytically, both reverently and with discrimination—with the devotion of a lover and the skill of a detective—if they desire to hear the Word of God in them.

Here are some of the ways this book differs from other introductions to Paul:

- It is intended to be brief, not encyclopedic, and chapters are intentionally short. But the style is concise and the sections compact, so the book will repay careful reading.

- It is written for ordinary Christian readers, not professional scholars. Technical vocabulary and scholarly footnotes have been kept to a minimum. Most footnotes contain only biblical references.

- It focuses on Paul's message and its relevance for us today, not on the critical questions that dominate scholarly discussion[2] and the New Perspective on Paul.[3]

- It highlights the ways Paul's experience of Christ transformed his life and thinking as a Jew. While taking seriously the influence of his Jewish background, the book focuses rather on the ways his traditional Jewish outlook was changed by Christ.[4]

---

2. Among others, these include questions about (1) the authorship, dating, and literary integrity (unity) of the letters; (2) the historical origins, theological center, and development of Paul's thought; (3) Paul's use of the Old Testament; and (4) the comparison of Paul and Jesus.

3. The New Perspective on Paul represents a variety of recent perspectives, all of which challenge the traditional interpretation of Paul—his perspectives on the gospel, the role of the Law in Judaism, "the works of the Law," "the righteousness of God," justification by faith, and political issues, among others. While the New Perspective has certainly resulted in useful insights, in my judgment some of its conclusions are less accurate than the traditional interpretation of Paul. Occasional comments in the book reflect my evaluation of some of the newer perspectives: see pp. 62 nn. 2, 3; 63 n. 6.

4. While traditional Jewish categories provide the framework of Paul's thought, his experience of Christ has filled this framework with new content. Christ's revelation to him marked a distinct break with much of his traditional understanding. Without denying the underlying continuity with his Old Testament heritage, the emphasis here is on the ways Paul came to see Christ as transcending much of traditional Judaism.

- It points up the ways Paul's life and thinking differ from—and challenge—the life and thinking of Christians today. The focus is on Paul's own agenda, not on our contemporary issues.

- It emphasizes the comprehensive, life-transforming nature of salvation in Paul's understanding—its power both to make people right with God and to change their lives, enabling them to overcome sin.

- It accentuates the paradoxical nature of Paul's theology—his twin emphases on God's sovereign work in salvation and the necessity of an individual's response.[5]

- It is based on the canonical Paul (all thirteen letters traditionally attributed to Paul[6]), not on the undisputed letters only.[7]

- It assumes that Luke's account of Paul's life in Acts of the Apostles provides reliable historical background for understanding Paul.[8]

This book is intended to be evangelical yet scholarly in its approach and constructive in its tone. The presumption throughout is that Paul's letters, as sacred Scripture, are to be taken with the utmost seriousness. My hope is that readers will find the book academically stimulating, theologically enriching, and personally challenging. Indeed, my greatest hope is that, through it, readers will find their appreciation of Christ and the gospel deepened and their Christian life reinvigorated and strengthened. This is what Paul would have wanted most.

Chapter 1 raises the question, why is Paul so important for us today? Chapters 2–3 then provide some background: an introduction to Paul's letters followed by an overview of his life. The rest of the book is devoted

5. Readers expecting Paul's thinking to be wholly consistent may find the paradoxical nature of his thought difficult to grasp. The opposing emphases occur side by side in his writings and cannot always be reconciled logically.

6. Some early Christians thought that Paul also wrote Hebrews, but few scholars today do.

7. Many scholars today would exclude 1 Timothy, 2 Timothy, and Titus as non-Pauline—and some would exclude Ephesians, Colossians, and 2 Thessalonians also (see comments on pp. 6–7). The analysis of Paul presented here is only minimally dependent on 2 Thessalonians, 1 Timothy, 2 Timothy, and Titus.

8. I assume the references to "we" in Acts 16–28 are not a literary device or quotations from someone else's diary, but probably derive from Luke himself. Perhaps one of Paul's own converts, Luke seems to have joined Paul's missionary team early in his second missionary trip; they then worked together for most of the rest of Paul's life. For a comprehensive defense of the historical reliability of Acts, see Hemer, *The Book of Acts.*

to his message, his theological ideas, and lessons we can learn from his life and thought. Attention is drawn at the end of each chapter to ways that Paul's life and thinking differ from the life and thinking of many Christians today. The final chapter summarizes the most important points and the challenge Paul poses to us. A brief summary and outline of each of the letters is included at the end.

The extensive biblical references in the footnotes provide more than documentation; they also serve as a resource for the study of related passages. Additional cross-references can be found in any good study Bible or commentary.

Biblical quotations are typically from my own translation of the Greek text.

In some chapters, I have drawn on ideas expressed in some of my previous writings. Readers interested in fuller expositions may wish to consult these.[9]

I am indebted to several colleagues and former students who graciously took the time to read and respond to these chapters. I am especially grateful to Jim Edwards, Greg Graybill, Gordon Jackson, Dottie Mohrlang, Jonathan Moo, Adam Neder, and Jerry Sittser, who read the entire manuscript and gave me invaluable critique. I am also thankful to Keith Beebe, Vic Bobb, Eric Brewer, Brian Dodd, Rich Erickson, Daniel Kaufman, and Charlie Nelson, who read select portions and gave me helpful comments and suggestions. The remaining inadequacies and failings are mine.

I would also like to thank Whitworth University for the grant of a Summer Research Fellowship and a Weyerhaeuser Fellowship, which provided funding for this project.

Now, settle down for a good read and enjoy getting to know this remarkable man and his revolutionary message for the world.

---

9. See Mohrlang, *Matthew and Paul*, "Love," "Paul," and "Romans."

1

Why is Paul So Important for Us Today?

"Especially make yourself familiar with Paul. Him you ought to hold ever in your heart, 'day and night he should dwell in your hand,' and his words you should commit to memory."

—ERASMUS

WHAT IS IT THAT makes Paul such a significant figure in the Christian faith? And why should we concern ourselves with him today, two thousand years later? Apart from the fact that his letters make up a large part of New Testament Scripture, here are some of the more obvious reasons:

HIS HISTORICAL SIGNIFICANCE

As the early church's most prominent missionary, Paul was the key figure in the explosive spread of the Christian faith in the first century; he spearheaded the Jesus movement. More than anyone else, Paul opened the Roman world to the message of Christ. Traipsing all over the northeastern end of the Mediterranean Basin—from Jerusalem all the way around to Illyricum (modern-day Albania)[1] and beyond—Paul was the first to proclaim the gospel and organize groups of believers in many of the key cities.

1. Rom 15:19.

1

When the Christian faith later came to dominate the Roman Empire, it was due more to Paul and his hard work than to any other person. It is no exaggeration to say that Paul's missionary work was instrumental in shaping the history of the western world.

HIS THEOLOGICAL SIGNIFICANCE

Paul was the most significant early exponent of Jesus and the gospel, and the most influential theologian of the early church. Of all the New Testament writers, it is Paul who gives us the fullest understanding of many of the key elements of Christian theology—human sinfulness, salvation, the cross, the Resurrection, justification by faith, the Holy Spirit, the church, the Christian life, and eschatology, among others. Not surprisingly, his writings played a key role in the formulation of the early Christian creeds. Apart from Jesus himself, Paul did more to shape the Jesus movement theologically than anyone else.[2]

Paul's references and allusions to the Old Testament also give us one of the clearest pictures of how the early Christians read and interpreted the Old Testament, and how they understood the relationship between the old and new covenants. As a result, his letters are important for anyone wishing to formulate a theology of the Bible as a whole.

HIS MISSIONARY SIGNIFICANCE

Paul's life reflects the priority the early church gave to evangelism. In obedience to the mandate given by Jesus himself, the missionary work of the early Christians focused on proclaiming the Good News of salvation and calling people to repent and embrace it; and this was the dominant focus of Paul's missionary work. All life long, he was driven to proclaim the gospel to those who had never heard it. The seriousness of his commitment to missionary evangelism has been an inspiration to Christians ever since and a key factor in the worldwide spread of the gospel. Many have taken Paul's way of doing missionary work as their model.

---

2. Paul's teachings have sometimes been set in contrast with those of Jesus; some scholars even think of Paul as the real founder of Christianity. For a comparison of Paul and Jesus that emphasizes their similarities, see Wenham, *Paul.*

HIS PASTORAL SIGNIFICANCE

Paul deals with a wider range of problems in the early church than any other New Testament writer. His letters give us the clearest view of the problems the early believers faced and the uniquely Christian way they were encouraged to deal with them. Here we find the most comprehensive pastoral advice in the New Testament. Especially significant is the extent to which his practical advice is rooted in the grace of God and the relationship of believers to Christ.[3]

These four reasons alone make Paul well worth serious study. He was a person of towering stature and significance in the early Christian movement. But an even more compelling reason beckons us to give him a serious reading today.

HIS SIGNIFICANCE FOR US PERSONALLY

The deepest significance of Paul for us lies in the astounding message he proclaims: the Good News that, through Jesus Christ, God *saves* us, undeserving though we are. Of all the New Testament writers, it is Paul who gives us the most comprehensive account of salvation in Christ. As we shall see in the coming chapters, this salvation is sweeping in its scope: it brings us both peace with God and life-transforming power. God not only forgives us, he also changes us. For those who feel the weight of their sins and failings, this message is extraordinarily good news.

Paul's life also serves as an incomparable example of what it means to be a committed servant of Christ. Once converted, he dedicated himself wholeheartedly to the service of the Savior. Embracing a life of suffering, he devoted the rest of his life to living—and ultimately dying—for Christ and his work in the world. His life serves as a model for anyone who desires to follow Christ seriously.

We should note at the beginning, however, that much of what Paul writes—much of his way of thinking and living—is distinctly different from our way of thinking and living as Christians today. And if we take the authority of Scripture seriously, that is troubling. If we take time to read Paul patiently and carefully, we shall begin to see just how different his thoughts are from ours. As troubling as they are, however, these

3. See chapter 14.

3

differences challenge us to reevaluate our lives and thinking, and can bring us to a truer, deeper experience of Christ and the Christian life.

Significantly, when there have been strong movements of revival and renewal in the history of the church, the stimulus has often come from those whose lives have been transformed by these powerful letters. The sixteenth-century Protestant Reformation, the eighteenth-century Evangelical Revival, and the modern-day worldwide evangelical movement are noteworthy examples of the remarkable ways that God has worked through the words of Paul. Church history is replete with accounts of individuals whose lives have been converted and transformed by these words—Augustine, Luther, John and Charles Wesley, and Karl Barth, among countless others. There is life-changing *power* in these letters.

2

Paul's Letters: Introductory Issues

THE NATURE OF THE LETTERS

THROUGHOUT PAUL'S MISSIONARY CAREER, he was busy writing pastoral letters to the new groups of Christians left behind him, which typically met in believers' homes.[1] These letters were intended to encourage and strengthen the believers in their new life in Christ and to give them advice on various problems they were facing. He also wrote letters to individual Christian leaders, including his missionary associates. Filled with his theological insight, pastoral wisdom, and passion for Christ, these letters are an invaluable legacy Paul has left us.

The letters cover a wide range of issues (theological, moral, ecclesiastical, personal, and interpersonal) and give us an unparalleled window into the life and problems of the earliest Christian home fellowships. They also give us a window into the Christ-centered thinking and pastoral heart of Paul himself, and his understanding of the gospel.

When we study Paul's letters, then, we focus on two levels: (1) the specific problems and issues the early Christians faced, together with Paul's perspectives on them, and (2) his theological thinking as a whole. In all our study, however, we must remember that much of what he wrote is not abstract theology but advice for specific issues that must be interpreted contextually.

1. Rom 16:5; 1 Cor 16:19; Col 4:15; Phlm 2.

Four of the letters (Romans, Galatians, Ephesians, and Colossians) display a similar two-part structure: (1) a section on the gospel followed by (2) a section on the Christian life. In three of these letters,[2] the second section is an explicit response to the first. This structure reflects Paul's view of the Christian life as an expression of gratitude to God for the grace shown in the gospel.[3]

The sheer number of Paul's letters in the New Testament expresses the important role he played in the early Christian community. Thirteen of the twenty-seven New Testament writings are attributed to him.[4] Paul's letters were among the first Christian writings to be recognized as New Testament Scripture. Paul also wrote other letters, which have never been found, including two additional letters to the church in Corinth and one to the church in Laodicea.[5]

The letters vary in the care with which they were written. Some, like Romans, are well thought out and carefully organized. Second Corinthians, on the other hand, is more fragmented and difficult to follow. (Like Galatians, it was written in the heat of emotion.) The fact that some of the longer letters may have been written over several days may contribute to the sense of fragmentation. We must remember that Paul wrote these letters in precomputer days, without the aid of a delete button and easy means of revision.

At least some of the letters were written with the aid of a scribe,[6] with Paul sometimes taking the quill in hand to add a few words in his own handwriting at the end.[7] What we don't know is how much freedom scribes had in Paul's day to express their clients' ideas in their own words. We cannot assume that they were bound to strict dictation.

QUESTIONS ABOUT AUTHENTICITY AND CONSISTENCY

Questions are frequently raised about the authenticity of some of the letters—especially 1 Timothy, 2 Timothy, and Titus, but sometimes Ephesians, Colossians, and 2 Thessalonians also. Some scholars think the

2. Romans, Ephesians, and Colossians.

3. See pp. 108–9.

4. See pp. 6–7.

5. 1 Cor 5:9; 2 Cor 2:3–4; 7:8, 12; Col 4:16.

6. Rom 16:22.

7. 1 Cor 16:21; Gal 6:11; Col 4:18; 2 Thess 3:17.

differences in theological content, vocabulary, and style of these letters are sufficient to demonstrate that they were written not by Paul but by a later disciple writing in the Apostle's name. But if we make allowance for (1) Paul's use of co-authors and scribes, and the freedom scribes may have had to put his ideas into their own words, (2) the widely varying issues he was required to address over the years, and (3) the ordinary differences reflected in any individual's writings over so many years, then the argument for non-Pauline authorship loses much of its force.[8] Even if some of the Greek manuscripts do reflect the touch of later editors, there is no compelling reason to conclude that the letters don't substantially derive from Paul himself and don't reflect the essence of his thought. So all thirteen letters (the classic Pauline canon) are included in this analysis. This is a study of the *canonical* Paul.

Questions are also raised about the consistency of Paul's letters. However, it is important to remember that these letters are not precisely worded philosophical essays but ordinary letters using language in ordinary, sometimes loose ways that easily leave the impression of inconsistency. The following all contribute to this impression:

- his overstatements, especially in arguments or highly emotional passages;[9]

- his contrasting emphases, addressed to quite different issues;[10]

- his paradoxical way of theological thinking, with its dual emphasis on God's sovereign choice in salvation and the necessity of personal response;[11]

- the development of his thinking about certain issues (for example, marriage and the single life).[12]

But we need not conclude that Paul's thought is radically inconsistent. While leaving room for the paradoxical nature of his thinking and the loose ends that characterize most ordinary writing, this book judges Paul's thought and writings to be both coherent and consistent overall. Further,

---

8. For a well-reasoned argument for the Pauline authorship of the Pastoral Letters, see Kelly, *The Pastoral Epistles*, 27–34.

9. Such statements frequently include the words "all," "every," "everyone," "everything," "none," "no one," "nothing," "not any."

10. See, for example, his statements about the Law (pp. 71–77), the dual nature of the believer's life (pp. 85–86), sin and the power of the Spirit (pp. 44–46), and the afterlife (pp. 133–35).

11. See chapter 8; cf. pp. 48–49 on the question of why the Jews are not saved.

12. See 1 Cor 7:39–40; 1 Tim 5:11–15; cf. pp. 134–35 on the timing of the afterlife.

there is little evidence of any major development in his theological beliefs over the years.

WHEN WERE THE LETTERS WRITTEN?

Paul's letters are not arranged in chronological order but are divided into two groups: (1) letters to churches (Romans–2 Thessalonians) and (2) letters to individuals (1 Timothy–Philemon). Each of these groups is ordered roughly according to the length of its letters, from longest to shortest. These thirteen letters were written over a period of perhaps no more than seventeen years, during the latter part of Paul's missionary career (about AD 48–65). When correlated with Luke's account of Paul's life in Acts, most of them can be given an approximate date. A few (Galatians and the Prison Letters especially), however, are difficult to date with any degree of precision.

Here are the approximate dates for each letter, as assumed in this book:

after 48–49   Galatians (written sometime after Paul's first mission trip and the meeting in Jerusalem described in Acts 15[13])

50–52   1, 2 Thessalonians (written near the end of Paul's second mission trip)

52–57   1, 2 Corinthians; Romans—and possibly Ephesians, Philippians, Colossians, and Philemon[14] (written during Paul's third mission trip)

59–65   1, 2 Timothy; Titus[15] (written sometime after Paul's original arrival in Rome)

A brief summary and outline of each of the thirteen letters is provided at the end of the book.

13. I assume the Jerusalem meeting recounted in Gal 2:1–10 is the same as that described in Acts 15. Some scholars link it rather to the visit to Jerusalem described in Acts 11:27–30.

14. Ephesians, Philippians, Colossians, and Philemon are called the Prison Letters. Written from prison, in my judgment they are best dated to the difficult time Paul experienced in the Roman province of Asia (western Turkey), AD 52–56 (see 2 Cor 1:8–9; 11:23–28, written shortly after his leaving the province). Alternatively, some or all of them may have been written during Paul's later imprisonment in Rome, nearer the end of his life.

15. 1 Timothy, 2 Timothy, and Titus are called the Pastoral Letters, and are among the latest of Paul's letters.

3

An Overview of Paul's Life

HIS BACKGROUND

IN THE PROVIDENCE OF God, Paul was given a multicultural background well suited to his future calling. Reared in an orthodox Jewish home in Tarsus,[1] a distinguished Greek university city in the Roman province of Cilicia (southeastern Turkey), he grew up speaking Greek (the lingua franca of the eastern Mediterranean world)[2] and knowing Greek culture. He also had the distinct advantage of inheriting Roman citizenship, with all its rights and privileges.[3] This multicultural background was to serve him well in his missionary travels in the Greco-Roman world.

---

1. Acts 9:11; 21:39; 22:3; cf. 9:30.

2. Acts 21:37. His letters are written in Greek and his quotations of Scripture are generally from the Greek version of the Old Testament (the Septuagint). He also apparently learned Aramaic, the mother tongue of Palestinian Jews. (This is the probable meaning of the word translated as "Hebrew" in Acts 21:40; 22:2.)

3. Acts 16:37–39; 22:25–29; 23:27. Neither Luke nor Paul tells us how or why his family received Roman citizenship. Jerome records the tradition of Paul's parents being carried off as prisoners of war from the Galilean town of Gischala to Tarsus, where they were sold as slaves and then later freed and given Roman citizenship: *De Viris Illistribus,* chapter V.

Above all, however, Paul was thoroughly Jewish. Born into a family with roots in the tribe of Benjamin[4] and given the name Saul[5] (Paulus was his Roman name, used in his travels in the Roman Empire[6]), he was brought up by parents who identified themselves as Pharisees.[7] As such, the family was committed to the serious study and interpretation of the Law of Moses. Their dedication to the Torah even led them to send their son away in his youth for training by one of Jerusalem's best-known rabbis, Gamaliel.[8] Paul later proudly spoke of himself in those days as "a pure-blooded Hebrew, a Pharisee in matters of the Law."[9]

Thoroughly immersed in Pharisaic culture, Paul developed a zealous passion for the purity and religious traditions of Judaism—and a fanatical hostility to the new Jesus movement and its rapidly growing number of converts.[10] The account of Paul's pre-Christian days in Acts of the Apostles portrays him as a holy terror—aggressively chasing down Christians (women as well as men), violently dragging them from their homes, tying them up for incarceration and punishment, and doing everything he could to force them to deny their faith in Christ.[11] Just how seriously he took the threat of this new "heretical" movement can be seen in the lengths to which he went to track down Christians and get them arrested—even as far away as Damascus (135 miles northeast of Jerusalem). His persecuting rage was driven by his Jewish concern to maintain the purity of God's truth and God's ways.

HIS CONVERSION AND EARLY MINISTRY

According to Acts, it was in the course of Paul's violent persecution of Christians that he came to the turning point of his life, his dramatic conversion. On his way to chase down Christians in Damascus, he was suddenly

---

4. Rom 11:1; Phil 3:5.

5. His namesake King Saul, also from the tribe of Benjamin, was the first king of Israel.

6. Luke first uses the name *Paulus* in Acts 13:9. The common belief that *Paul* was the Apostle's Christian name has no basis.

7. Acts 23:6.

8. Acts 22:3.

9. Phil 3:5; cf. Acts 26:5; 2 Cor 11:22.

10. Acts 8:1–3; 9:1–2; 22:3–5; 26:9–11; 1 Cor 15:9; Gal 1:13–14; Phil 3:6.

11. Acts 7:58; 8:1, 4; 9:1; 22:4–5; 26:9–11; cf. 1 Cor 15:9; Gal 1:13–14; Phil 3:6; 1 Tim 1:13.

confronted by the resurrected Christ himself. Paul was astounded to learn that the voice he was hearing from heaven was that of Jesus, and that Jesus was calling him to be his witness and messenger to the world. The experience changed him forever. From that moment on, Paul realized that his life was claimed by Christ and must be devoted to him.[12]

After a brief trip to the desert area east of Damascus[13] (either a retreat to deepen his understanding and experience of the Lord or an initial evangelistic foray), he immediately began to tell others in Damascus about Christ. He soon encountered (first in Damascus, then in Jerusalem) the same kind of hostility from fellow Jews that he himself had inflicted on the followers of Jesus. Coming to his rescue, the Christian leaders in Jerusalem hurriedly took him down to the coast, put him on board a ship, and sent him back to his original home, Tarsus, to save his life.[14]

We know nothing of Paul's life or work during the next ten to fourteen years. Then a well-respected evangelist by the name of Barnabas, who had earlier struck up a friendship with Paul, tracked him down and persuaded him to join him in teaching the large community of gentile converts in the Syrian metropolis of Antioch, the site of the first large-scale conversion of gentiles. (It was there that the followers of Jesus were first called Christians.) The two men spent a whole year discipling the new converts and then took a brief trip to Jerusalem to deliver a gift of money for the poverty-stricken believers there.[15]

HIS FIRST MISSION TRIP[16]

Paul and Barnabas were then called by the Holy Spirit to undertake a more extensive mission for Christ. Taking Barnabas's cousin John Mark with them, they left Antioch, preached their way across the island of Cyprus, then sailed to the southern coast of Turkey. There they preached in the coastal town of Perga, where John Mark inexplicably left them. Then they climbed to the inland plateau and preached the message of Christ in four nearby towns: Antioch, Iconium, Lystra, and Derbe. Paul's typical pattern was to begin by preaching in the local synagogue, where both Jews and gentile converts to Judaism would be found, and then turn to the gentiles

---

12. Acts 9:1–19; 22:6–16; 26:12–18.

13. "Arabia" (Gal 1:17); Luke makes no mention of this trip in Acts.

14. Acts 9:20–30.

15. Acts 11:25–30.

16. Acts 13:1—14:28.

when the Jews became hostile. It was not an easy time; they encountered opposition (sometimes severe) throughout the trip. Nevertheless, through their preaching a nucleus of new believers came together in each town. Returning the way they had come, Paul and Barnabas encouraged the believers and appointed leaders in each church. Then they sailed back to their home church in Antioch of Syria, where they reported how God had used them to bring about the conversion of gentiles.

THE DECISION IN JERUSALEM[17]

Not long after that, however, because of the growing number of gentile converts in Antioch, a fierce argument arose over whether gentile believers should be circumcised and taught to observe the Law of Moses, as many Jewish believers insisted. Because obedience to the Law was such an important and emotional issue to Jews, the church decided to send a delegation up to Jerusalem, to thrash the question out with the original Christian leaders there. They selected Paul and Barnabas to lead the delegation. What followed was a full-blown discussion of the issue with the Christian leaders in Jerusalem, resulting in the crucial conclusion that they would *not* impose circumcision and other rituals of the Law of Moses on gentile believers—to the great relief of the gentile Christians in Antioch. This decision effectively gave official endorsement to the mission of Paul and Barnabas among the gentiles.

HIS SECOND MISSION TRIP[18]

Paul's second mission trip from Antioch was undertaken with Silas, a Jewish Christian from Jerusalem, after a strong argument between Paul and Barnabas over John Mark resulted in a breakup of the original team.[19] (Whether the sheer strength of Paul's personality and convictions[20] was a factor in the breakup of the relationship is not clear.) After visiting and encouraging the churches begun on the first trip and inviting a promising young disciple by the name of Timothy to join them, Paul and Silas

17. Acts 15:1–35.

18. Acts 15:36—18:22.

19. The rift between Paul and John Mark was later overcome: Col 4:10; 2 Tim 4:11; Phlm 24.

20. See Gal 1:8–9; 5:12; note the strong tone of 2 Corinthians 10–13 and Galatians especially; cf. Acts 21:12–14.

attempted to cross into the Roman provinces of Asia (western Turkey) and Bithynia (northern Turkey). But sensing the Spirit was opposing their plans, they decided to proceed instead down to the town of Troas on the coast (northwestern Turkey). That night Paul had a vision that convinced them that God was calling them to the Roman province of Macedonia (northeastern Greece). After crossing the Aegean Sea, they proceeded to engage in evangelistic work in some of the main Macedonian towns close to the coast (Philippi, Thessalonica, and Berea). A group of believers was successfully planted in each town, but in each place so much opposition arose that they quickly had to move on. After a brief time of preaching farther south in Athens (the old center of classical Greece), Paul made his way down the coast of the Roman province of Achaia (southern Greece) to the key port city of Corinth, where he was finally able to settle down for an extended period (eighteen months) of evangelism.[21] But there too he encountered considerable antagonism. At the end of that time, with Silas accompanying him, Paul returned again to the church in Syrian Antioch that had originally sent him out.

HIS THIRD MISSION TRIP[22]

Paul's third mission trip targeted the large port city of Ephesus on the western coast of the Roman province of Asia (western Turkey). There he spent two to three years preaching the Good News, not only in Ephesus but also throughout the province. Again, he seems to have encountered hostility wherever he went; it was an extremely difficult time. In 2 Corinthians, written shortly after he left the province, Paul speaks of imprisonments, whippings, beatings, an experience of stoning, and frequent difficulties, dangers, and threats to his life.[23] Finally, because of an uproar over the negative economic impact of his preaching on silversmiths making shrines devoted to the goddess Artemis, he decided it was time to leave the province. He then revisited each of the churches that he had helped to plant along the eastern coast of Macedonia and Achaia several years earlier. When he heard word of a plot to assassinate him in Achaia, he decided it was safer to retreat with his missionary team[24] back north

21. In Corinth Paul stayed with Priscilla and Aquila, who were tent-makers like himself: Acts 18:2–3.

22. Acts 18:23—21:16.

23. 2 Cor 11:23–29; cf. 1:8–9.

24. Acts 20:4.

through Macedonia than to go directly on to Syria. Later, after a moving farewell to the leaders of the newly established church in Ephesus, Paul finally boarded a ship for Syria, convinced that God was calling him to Jerusalem—despite the worries of Christians along the way about his safety, and the conviction of some that the trip was not God's will.[25]

HIS IMPRISONMENT IN JUDEA AND TRIP TO ROME[26]

Within a week of his arrival in Jerusalem with a sizeable gift of money collected from gentile believers for the poor believers in the city,[27] Paul was mobbed and almost killed by an angry crowd in the Temple, stirred up by Jews from the province of Asia who opposed him. He was barely rescued by the battalion of Roman soldiers posted to the Temple area. When the Roman commander then learned of a Jewish plot to kill Paul, he decided to transfer him immediately from Jerusalem down to the Roman fort on the coast at Caesarea for safekeeping. Paul spent the next two years confined to the fort, though he took advantage of every opportunity to speak about Christ with the Roman and Jewish officials he encountered there. When a newly appointed procurator proposed that his case be tried in Jerusalem, Paul—aware of the dangers facing him in Jerusalem and perhaps sensing a divine opportunity—requested that his case be transferred to Rome, in view of his Roman citizenship.

Accordingly, he was put on board a ship with some other prisoners and sent off to Rome in the custody of a Roman army officer. Luke and another Christian friend, Aristarchus, accompanied him. On the way, their lives were miraculously spared in a shipwreck off the coast of Malta. When Paul finally arrived in Rome, he was placed under house arrest but was allowed to share Christ freely with all those who came to see him. He was still there two years later—and that is where Luke's account of Paul's life strangely breaks off (probably because that is when Luke wrote Acts). We are left wondering about the outcome of his case.

25. By this time, Paul felt his work in the northeastern end of the Mediterranean region was finished, and he was making plans to travel to Spain, in the Latin-speaking western end of the region. First, however, he wanted to deliver the money he had been collecting for the poor Christians in Jerusalem: Rom 15:23–29.

26. Acts 21:17—28:31.

27. Rom 15:25–28; 1 Cor 16:1–4; 2 Cor 8–9.

HIS FINAL YEARS

There are two traditions that relate to Paul's life after this time, and both may be regarded as reliable. One tradition comes from Clement, an elder in the church in Rome who, in a letter to the church in Corinth, wrote (about AD 95) that Paul eventually reached "the farthest limits of the West"[28]—commonly understood to mean Spain, where Paul had long been wanting to do missionary work.[29] In support of this tradition, good reasons exist to believe that his case would have been dismissed when it finally came to trial in Rome, freeing him for further missionary work. Roman officials had already acknowledged that they had no real case against him.[30] Moreover, as an elder in the church of Rome, writing within thirty years of Paul's death in the city, Clement would almost certainly have known what happened to Paul. Unfortunately, we have no account of Paul's life or the specific work he did in the western Mediterranean area.

A second tradition, equally reliable, speaks of Paul dying in Rome, together with Peter, during the persecution of Nero in the mid-60s AD.[31] Exactly when, where, and why he was rearrested is not known. In any case, just as he had longed to live for Christ, so he had longed to die for Christ[32]—and was finally given the privilege of doing so. The sacrifice of his life in the service of Christ was the culmination of his lifelong dedication to the Savior, to whose mercy he owed everything.

28. Clement, "The Letter of the Romans to the Corinthians," 35.

29. Rom 15:23–28. Some scholars, however, interpret the phrase "the farthest limits of the West" as a reference to Rome itself, although Clement (writing from Rome) almost certainly would not have described the city that way. Spain was a long-established and integral part of the Roman Empire by this time, and "the farthest limits of the West" would almost certainly have referred to *Hispania Ulterior* (farther Spain, or western Spain): Greg Graybill, personal memo.

30. Acts 25:24–27; cf. 26:31–32.

31. Eusebius, *The History of the Church*, sec. 2.25, citing Gaius of Rome and Dionysius of Corinth.

32. Phil 3:10.

4

The Beginning of It All
Paul's Encounter with Jesus

To UNDERSTAND PAUL, WE must first appreciate the significance of his highly unusual conversion and its radical impact on his life. His encounter with the resurrected Christ was the great turning point of his life, the event that changed all his thinking about Jesus and revolutionized his life. We cannot understand Paul apart from the experience of his conversion.

HIS CONVERSION

According to Luke's account in Acts, it was in the course of Paul's violent attacks on Christians that the momentous event happened. With a letter from the chief priest in his satchel, authorizing him to chase down Jewish converts to Christ in Damascus, he was abruptly halted on the way by a voice confronting him from heaven, the voice of the resurrected Lord. Though Luke's details are few, all three of his accounts of the event[1] relate Paul's clear sense that it was Jesus himself who was challenging him: "'Saul, Saul,[2] why are you persecuting me?' 'Who are you, Lord?' he replied. 'I am Jesus, the one you are persecuting!'" (Acts 9:4–5; cf. 22:7–8; 26:14–5).

---

1. Acts 9:1–19; 22:6–16; 26:12–18.
2. For an explanation of Paul's two names, see p. 10.

In this frightening confrontation, which according to Luke left Paul blinded for three days,[3] Christ not only called Paul to account, but also, incredibly, summoned his former antagonist to be his witness and messenger to the gentile world.[4] This traumatic encounter turned Paul's life upside down. It was his great moment of truth, and it called into question much of what he had believed and lived for as a devout student of the Law. From that moment on, aware of the divine mercy shown to him, Paul knew that Christ had claimed his life for himself, and that the rest of his days must be devoted to serving him. He became as zealous an advocate of Jesus as he had been a persecutor of his followers. Everything changed when he came to realize who Jesus is.

HIS VIEW OF JESUS [5]

By way of background, we must remember that for many years devout Jews had been looking forward to the coming of the Kingdom of God—the day when God would come to establish his rule in the world, fulfill the biblical promises, free his people from those who oppressed them, and make everything right. They longed for the time of ultimate justice, righteousness, peace, and blessing that the Prophets had predicted.

The arrival of that day was to be marked by the coming of the long-awaited Messiah—the king sent by God to establish his rule in the world, the promised Son of David.[6] Many Jews anticipated a return of the golden days of King David, a time of widespread peace and prosperity brought about by a powerful descendant of the great king who would rule from Jerusalem. Although messianic expectations varied in Judaism, many Jews seem to have thought of the Messiah as a victorious military commander like David who would drive the Romans out by force and restore Jewish independence after centuries of colonial oppression. Jesus, a criminal executed by the Romans on a cross, clearly did not meet those military and political expectations.

But as a result of his experience with the resurrected Christ, Paul was compelled to acknowledge that this dead "heretic" was indeed the Messiah. How much of his later understanding of Jesus was the direct result

3. Acts 9:8–9.

4. Acts 13:47; 22:21; 26:17–18; Rom 1:5; 11:13; 15:15–18; Gal 1:16; 2:7–9; Eph 3:1, 8; 1 Tim 2:7; see pp. 140–41.

5. This section reflects ideas found in Mohrlang, "Paul."

6. 2 Sam 7:16; Ps 89:19–37; 132:11–12; Isa 9:6–7; 11:1–10.

of Jesus's revelation to him, and how much the result of reflection on its implications or what he learned from earlier Christians, is difficult to say. But there is no disputing that Paul's life and thinking were dramatically reoriented because of his new understanding of the Lord.

So how did Paul come to think of Jesus? Who exactly did he understand him to be, and how does he portray him in his letters?

SON OF GOD AND MESSIAH

Luke says that from his earliest days as a convert, Paul proclaimed to the Jews that Jesus is the *Son of God*,[7] the *Messiah*,[8] supporting his claims from Scripture.[9] In Paul's letters, these two terms are closely related (as they are in the gospels[10]).

As Son of God[11] (a term used of royalty throughout the ancient Mediterranean world, and in early Judaism increasingly of the royal heir, the great Davidic king to come, the promised Messiah[12]), Jesus stands in a unique relationship to God, with divinely given authority, power, and privilege. His Resurrection from the dead confirms his unique status.[13] As Son of God, he is to be supremely honored. As Son of God, Jesus also expresses the greatness of God's redemptive love: the one whom God sacrificed for the sins of the world is no one less than his own Son. (And if his love moved him to do *that*, Paul reasons, surely God will provide for all the other needs of his chosen people.[14]) Jesus's sacrificial death also expresses the greatness of the Son's own love.[15] Moreover, as God's Son, he is now the elder brother of all those who become God's adopted children (sons) by embracing him.[16]

---

7. Acts 9:20.

8. Acts 9:22.

9. See Acts 17:2–3, 11.

10. Cf. Matt 16:16; 26:63; Luke 4:41; John 11:27; 20:31.

11. In Greek, *huios tou theou*; Rom 1:3, 4, 9; 5:10; 8:3, 29, 32; 1 Cor 1:9; 15:28; 2 Cor 1:19; Gal 1:16; 2:20; 4:4, 6; Eph 4:13; Col 1:13; 1 Thess 1:10.

12. Cf. Ps 2:7: "You are my son; today I have become your father," quoted by Paul in Acts 13:32–33; cf. Ps 89:26–27; Heb 1:5; 5:5. This was in accordance with God's original promise to King David: 2 Sam 7:14.

13. Rom 1:4.

14. Rom 8:32; cf. 5:5, 8, 10; 8:31–39.

15. Gal 2:20.

16. Rom 8:29; cf. Gal 4:4–5.

As Messiah,[17] he is the long-awaited one who has come to fulfill the promises God made to his people long ago.[18] He is the culmination of God's redemptive work that began in Genesis.[19] As Messiah, he is the Son of David who has come to establish God's rule over the gentiles as well as the Jews.[20] He is the heaven-sent king who has now inaugurated the Kingdom of God. But this is quite a different kind of kingdom from the military kingdom established by David, the kind of kingdom many Jews expected the Messiah to establish. In its present form, the Kingdom of God is the rule of God in the hearts of those who yield their lives to him and embrace his Messiah; it is a spiritual kingdom, not a political kingdom.[21] Although the full eschatological experience of the Kingdom awaits the future return of Jesus, those who submit to God's rule can begin to experience the life and power of his Kingdom here and now.[22]

Significantly, Paul speaks much more of the Kingdom of God than the Kingdom of Christ,[23] and only once refers explicitly to Jesus as king.[24] Moreover, when he addresses gentile converts, he doesn't emphasize Jesus's role as Messiah and king so much as his roles as Lord and Savior; these are the most important roles of Christ for Paul's missionary work in the Greco-Roman world.

LORD

Paul speaks more than two hundred times of Jesus as *Lord*.[25] As Lord, Jesus is the ultimate master of everyone and everything, the ruler of the universe who will one day be the final judge of every person.[26] Only those who confess him as the resurrected Lord will be saved: "If you confess that

17. In Greek, *Christos,* "anointed one," a translation of the Hebrew word *māšîah.* In his letters, Paul often (but not always) seems to use the word *Christ* simply as Jesus's name, reflecting early Christian usage.

18. Rom 15:8.

19. Gen 12:1–3.

20. Rom 15:12.

21. Rom 14:17; cf. John 18:36: "My kingdom is not an earthly kingdom."

22. See pp. 84–85.

23. Paul refers to the Kingdom of Christ only four times: 1 Cor 15:24–25; Eph 5:5; Col 1:13; 2 Tim 4:1.

24. 1 Tim 6:15; cf. Acts 17:7.

25. In Greek, *kyrios.*

26. 2 Cor 5:10; 2 Tim 4:1; cf. Rom 2:16; 1 Cor 4:5. Other New Testament references to Christ as final judge include John 5:27; Acts 10:42.

Jesus is Lord and believe in your heart that God raised him from death, you will be saved" (Rom 10:9).[27]

But the confession of Jesus as Lord must be more than a mere formal acknowledgment of who he is. As we shall see later, it must be an expression of a believer's personal submission to him as his or her own master.[28] As Lord, Jesus deserves the wholehearted devotion of every believer; everything a Christian does is to be done for the Lord,[29] as his slave.[30]

Because he shares the title of Lord with God,[31] Jesus deserves the same honor as God himself. Although Paul only rarely speaks explicitly of Jesus as God,[32] Jesus and God share the same characteristics and fill similar roles in his letters. Like God, Jesus has existed from the very beginning. The entire universe was created through him and for him, and he is the one who sustains it.[33] His authority transcends that of all other spiritual powers.[34] Jesus had the nature of God before coming to earth, gave up his privileged position to come and die as a sacrifice for sin, and after his Resurrection returned to his glorified position in the presence of God.[35] There he now intercedes for his people, just as his Spirit does within them.[36] One day he will triumph over all his enemies[37] and stand as the final judge of all.[38] And on that day, every knee—of the living and dead alike, of unbelievers as well as believers—will bow before him, and every being in the universe will acknowledge that he is the Lord.[39] As the living embodiment of all that God is ("In Christ, the full nature of God

27. Cf. Rom 10:13; 1 Cor 12:3.

28. See pp. 110–11; cf. Rom 14:7–9; 2 Cor 5:14–15; Col 3:17.

29. Eph 5:22; 6:5–7; Col 3:22–24; cf. 1 Cor 7:32–35.

30. Rom 1:1; 14:4; 1 Cor 7:22; Gal 1:10; Eph 6:5–6, 9; Phil 1:1; Col 3:22–24; 4:1, 24; 2 Tim 2:24; Titus 1:1; cf. Rom 14:7–18. Greek *doulos,* "slave," may also be translated "servant" or "bond-servant."

31. The Hebrew words *yhwh* and *ʾădōnāy* are both translated as *kyrios* in the Greek version of the Old Testament. These Hebrew words are translated as "LORD" and "Lord" respectively in most English versions.

32. Rom 9:5; Titus 2:13; cf. 2 Thess 1:12.

33. 1 Cor 8:6; Col 1:15–17.

34. Eph 1:20–22; Col 2:10, 15; cf. 1 Cor 15:24–25.

35. Phil 2:6–11; Col 3:1; cf. Ps 110:1; 1 Cor 10:4; 2 Cor 8:9.

36. Rom 8:26–27, 34; cf. Heb 7:25; 9:24; 1 John 2:1.

37. 1 Cor 15:24–27.

38. 2 Cor 5:10; cf. Rom 2:16; 14:10–12; 1 Cor 4:4–5.

39. Phil 2:9–11.

lives in a human body," Col 2:9), Jesus is supreme over all[40] and completely sufficient for salvation.[41]

Paul's view of Jesus as divine is also reflected in the following:

- the pairing of the names of Jesus and God in his beginning invocations ("May God our Father and the Lord Jesus Christ give you grace and peace")[42]

- the use of Jesus's name in his closing benedictions ("May the grace of our Lord Jesus Christ be with you")[43]

- his reference to being commissioned "by Jesus Christ and God the Father"[44]

- his phrase "the Kingdom of Christ and of God"[45]

- his transformation of the Old Testament eschatological "day of the Lord" into the "day of Christ"[46]

- his Christological interpretation of Old Testament texts referring to God[47]

Clearly, Paul thinks of Jesus as sharing in the nature of God himself. The Creator has become the Savior.

But Paul still understands Jesus as ultimately subordinate to God the Father in the divine hierarchy—that is, subordinate in position, not in essence.[48] He is, after all, the ever-obedient *Son* of God.[49] In the end, he will bow his own knee to God his Father.[50] Here we see something of the complexity that later Christians had to wrestle with as they struggled to verbalize the relation of the divine Son to God the Father in Trinitarian terms.

---

40. Col 1:15–20; 2:17.

41. Col 2:9–15; cf. 2 Cor 5:19.

42. Rom 1:7; 1 Cor 1:3; 2 Cor 1:2; Gal 1:3; Eph 1:2; Phil 1:2; Col 1:2; 2 Thess 1:2; 1 Tim 1:2; 2 Tim 1:2; Titus 1:4; Phlm 3; cf. 1 Thesss 1:1.

43. Rom 16:24; 1 Cor 16:23; 2 Cor 13:13; Gal 6:18; Eph 6:23; Phil 4:23; 1 Thess 5:28; 2 Thess 3:18; Phlm 25; cf. 2 Tim 4:22.

44. Gal 1:1.

45. Eph 5:5; cf. 1 Cor 15:24; Col 1:13; 2 Tim 4:1.

46. 1 Cor 1:8; 2 Cor 1:14; Phil 1:6; 2:16.

47. Phil 2:10–11; cf. Rom 10:13.

48. 1 Cor 3:23; 11:3.

49. Rom 1:4.

50. 1 Cor 15:24, 28.

Some scholars see Paul's emphasis on Jesus as Lord as his way of contesting the Roman claim that the emperor (Caesar) was Lord,[51] thus making a "theopolitical" statement: "If Jesus is Lord, Caesar is not."[52] The following statement of Paul is sometimes adduced as evidence of his political concern:

> Although people speak of "gods" in heaven and on earth—many so-called "gods" and "lords"—for us there is only one God, the Father who created everything and for whom we live, and one Lord, Jesus Christ, through whom all things were created and through whom we live. (1 Cor 8:5–6)

But Paul is probably alluding here to the polytheistic beliefs of the Greco-Roman world generally, rather than to the divinity of the emperor specifically. Nevertheless, because of the way people referred to the emperor as Lord and God,[53] Paul would certainly have been aware of the political implications of his emphasis on Jesus as Lord. Yet nowhere does he spell out these political implications. Nowhere does he draw an explicit contrast between the emperor and Jesus as Lord. And nowhere does he explicitly dispute the claims of the Imperial Cult. Nor do his statements or the overall tone of his letters seem to be political in their emphasis.

Indeed, Paul urges Christians to show honor and deference to political rulers as God-ordained authorities who serve the purposes of God in the world.[54] Near the end of his life—after suffering abuse from many of those in power—he still instructs Christians to submit to secular authorities as part of their witness to the world: "Tell them not to speak evil of anyone," he writes.[55] Although he would never have agreed with the idea of a divine emperor, Paul appears to have been careful not to criticize the emperor, at least publicly. In general, his concern is theological and evangelistic, not political. He is more concerned with the question of *who Jesus is* than with the question of *who the emperor is not*.

But there were inevitable political repercussions. The number of times charges were brought against Paul before Roman authorities suggests

51. Ancient inscriptions and literary texts refer to the "good news" of the emperor's birth and accession to power, and to the "salvation," "peace," and "justice" associated with his universal reign as "Lord."

52. See Wright, *Paul in Fresh Perspective*, 59–79.

53. The heyday of emphasis on the divinity of the emperor, however, came only in the second century, well after Paul's time: Hurtado, "Lord," 561.

54. Rom 13:1–7.

55. Titus 3:2.

how often his witness to Christ as Lord was interpreted as a threat to the normal order or a challenge to Roman law and belief in the supremacy of the emperor.[56] (Luke records charges against him of breaking the laws of the emperor by claiming there was another king by the name of Jesus.[57]) Even though he was not fundamentally political in his orientation, he knew from experience the political risk he was taking in proclaiming Jesus as Lord (as faithful Christians in difficult political situations have known ever since). Even though Paul doesn't draw out the political implications explicitly, the confession of Jesus as Lord does mean, implicitly, that Caesar is *not*. No one else, nothing else, must ever claim a believer's absolute allegiance.

There were also unintended social and economic repercussions. In Ephesus, his preaching caused a riot because of its negative impact on the business of the local silversmiths who were making shrines devoted to the goddess Artemis. Although Paul was exonerated from the charge of speaking against Artemis,[58] the claims of the gospel had both economic and religious repercussions that were clearly not appreciated by devotees of the goddess.[59] Similarly, earlier in Philippi, Paul's exorcism of a slave girl's demon and the resulting loss of her moneymaking abilities resulted in angry charges from her owners that got him badly beaten and thrown into jail.[60]

Sometimes the proclamation of Christ may have unintended but inevitable religious, political, economic, or social repercussions. In situations like these, Paul would encourage Christians to be gracious but always faithful in their confession of Christ as Lord, whatever the consequences.

SAVIOR

Paul highlights Jesus's role as Savior as much as his role as Lord. Although he doesn't frequently speak of Jesus as Savior per se,[61] his gospel is, above all, a message of salvation. And Jesus is the one through whom this salvation is mediated exclusively: "Through Christ, God was reconciling the

---

56. Acts 16:21: "They are teaching customs that go against our law; we are Roman citizens"; cf. 18:13.

57. Acts 17:7; cf. the charges against Jesus in John 19:12, 15.

58. Acts 19:37.

59. Acts 19:23–41.

60. Acts 16:16–24.

61. Greek, *sōtēr*; Acts 13:23; Eph 5:23; Phil 3:20; 2 Tim 1:10; Titus 1:4; 2:13; 3:6.

world to himself" (2 Cor 5:19). Indeed, Paul emphasizes, Jesus himself *is* the salvation of believers—their "righteousness, holiness, and freedom from sin."[62]

As we shall see later, Paul (along with the early Christians as a whole) seems to have come to understand Jesus's death on the cross in the light of Isaiah 53, as the atoning sacrifice for the world's sins. In Paul's letters, the deepest significance of Christ lies in his death more than in his earthly life (his miracles, acts of compassion, and teachings). For Paul, the cross lies at the very heart of the Good News; the gospel is always "the message of the cross." The focus of all his preaching and teaching was "Jesus Christ crucified."[63]

But the cross and the Resurrection always go together in Paul's writing; together they represent God's great act of salvation. The Resurrection was God's unique way of confirming both the truth of Jesus and his victory over sin, the world, Satan, and death.[64] Paul also speaks of the Resurrection as the key to a transformed life because the resurrected Lord now comes to live in the hearts of his people,[65] with all his life-changing power.

The work of Christ as Savior, then, centers on his death and Resurrection. Through these two great saving events, believers are made right with God and given new power for living.[66]

THE POINT . . .

It is impossible to understand Paul without an appreciation of his conversion and the radical impact it had on his life. Because of his encounter with the resurrected Christ, he came to the shocking realization that Jesus is *not* the heretical Galilean preacher he once thought him to be, but the Son of God, the long-awaited Messiah, the Savior and Lord of the world— indeed, the human expression of God himself. As a result, the Savior came to mean *everything* to him; Christ became his all-consuming passion. And Paul dedicated the rest of his life to living for the Lord and his work in the world. *Everything changed when he came to realize who Jesus is.*

---

62. 1 Cor 1:30.

63. 1 Cor 1:23–24; Gal 3:1; 6:14; Phil 2:8; Col 1:20.

64. Rom 6:18; 7:25; 8:2, 31–39; 1 Cor 15:57; Gal 1:4.

65. Gal 2:20; Col 1:27; cf. Jer 31:31–34; Ezek 36:25–27; Eph 3:17.

66. For a fuller explanation of the significance of the cross and the Resurrection, see chapter 5.

So it is with us: the Christian life begins with a real embrace of Jesus Christ. Our experience of Jesus may not be as dramatic as Paul's, but it must be no less authentic. Apart from a real personal commitment to Jesus, a person cannot truly be called a Christian.

Only when we grasp the significance of who Jesus is will our lives begin to become all that God wants them to be. Only when we comprehend what it means to call him *Savior* and *Lord,* when we understand that he is *God* himself and that he will one day be our final *judge*—only then will we fathom how indebted we are to him and realize that we dare neither live nor die without him. Only then will we realize that he must mean *everything* to us and that our lives must be wholly dedicated to his love and service. For us too, *everything will change when we come to realize who Jesus is.*

5

The Crux

Jesus's Death and Resurrection

FOR PAUL, GOD'S REDEMPTIVE work in Christ centers on two crucial historical events: Jesus's death and Resurrection. Of all the New Testament writers, Paul is the one who spells out their significance most fully. These two events lie at the very heart of the message he proclaimed to the world as God's Good News. But why are they of such critical importance?

JESUS'S DEATH [1]

As a zealous young defender of Jewish traditions, Paul almost certainly would have agreed with the Roman decision to execute Jesus. From his reading of the Law of Moses, he might even have interpreted Jesus's death by crucifixion as an expression of God's curse on him.[2]

But his experience of the resurrected Christ resulted in a radically different view of Jesus's death—as the ultimate sacrifice for sin, the supreme gift of God by which the sins of the world are forgiven and the world is reconciled to God.[3] "Christ died for our sins" (1 Cor 15:3)—this was the

---

1. This section reflects ideas found in Mohrlang, "Paul."

2. In Gal 3:13 Paul cites a biblical text that speaks of anyone nailed to a tree as being under a curse (Deut 21:23, Greek version).

3. Rom 3:24–25; 5:6–11; Gal 2:21; Eph 1:7; Col 1:13–14; 1 Thess 5 10; 1 Tim 2:5–6; cf. Titus 2:14.

heart of the Good News that he preached everywhere. The crucifixion that had formerly seemed to be the expression of God's judgment became for him the quintessential expression of God's love.

How did Paul come to such a different understanding? In Galatians, he emphasizes that it was Christ himself, not any human being, who revealed the Good News to him.[4] The understanding of Jesus's death as an atoning sacrifice, however, was not unique to Paul. It was the common understanding of the early Christian community, and it reflected Jesus's own understanding of his God-given mission.[5] Behind it lies the enigmatic passage in Isaiah 53 that speaks of an innocent person who dies so that others may be forgiven vicariously. This is the passage of Scripture, more than any other, that Jesus seems to have taken as his divine calling:

> He suffered and endured great pain for us,
> but we thought his suffering was punishment from God.
> He was wounded and crushed because of our sins;
> by taking our punishment, he made us completely well.
> All of us were like sheep that had wandered off.
> We had each gone our own way,
> but the LORD gave him the punishment we deserved . . .
> The LORD decided his servant would suffer as a sacrifice
> to take away the sin and guilt of others . . .
> Although he is innocent,
> he will take the punishment for the sin of others,
> so that many of them will no longer be guilty . . .
> Others thought he was a sinner,
> but he suffered for our sins and asked God to forgive us. (Isa 53:4–12 CEV)

Intriguingly, in postexilic Judaism Isaiah 53 does not seem to have been widely considered a messianic passage. It includes no reference to "the anointed one" (the king/Messiah), and its description of a suffering servant contrasts sharply with the traditional understanding of the Messiah as a victor.

But Isaiah 53 is almost certainly the passage that Paul is thinking of when he writes about Scripture predicting the atoning death of Christ.[6] For unbelievers, of course, the notion of Jesus's death by crucifixion being an atonement for sin was preposterous. The claim that an executed criminal was in reality the Savior of the world was patently absurd, and it

4. Gal 1:11–12.
5. Matt 20:28; 26:28.
6. 1 Cor 15:3.

must have made the early evangelists the butt of many jokes. This is why Paul speaks of the message of the cross as scandalous: "The message about Christ's death on the cross is ludicrous to those who are being lost . . . [it is] a message that is offensive to the Jews and ridiculous to the gentiles" (1 Cor 1:18, 23).

For believers, however, Christ's death for undeserving sinners was supremely precious, the consummate expression of God's love for a lost world: "God has shown us how much he loves us: Christ died for us while we were still sinners!" (Rom 5:8).[7]

How could one person's death on a cross have atoning significance for everyone else? Jesus's death was the ultimate expression of his perfect obedience to God, the obedience that satisfied all the demands of the Law. He thereby absorbed the curse of God that is on all those who disobey the Law,[8] and reconciled them to God. His life of perfect obedience overcame all the terrible consequences of Adam's disobedience.[9] As a result, those who trust in him are now reconciled with God and saved from the wrath of God's coming judgment.[10] God now views believers as righteous because of Christ's righteousness; his perfect righteousness is now credited to them.[11]

For Paul, the message of the cross represents the heart of the Christian faith and addresses people's deepest need. Moreover, he is convinced that this simple message has a power of its own to evoke faith and bring forgiveness to people convicted of their sins.[12] When he preaches the gospel, he does not rely simply on his own intellectual or rhetorical ability to convince people but on the power of the message itself to convert their hearts.[13]

According to Paul, Christ's death on the cross is what assures believers that God is fully for them and will provide for all their deepest needs forever:

> With God on our side, who could possibly stand against us?
> Certainly not God, who did not even keep back his own Son
> but gave him up for us all! And if he gave us his Son, will he

---

7. Cf. Eph 2:4–5.

8. Gal 3:13; cf. Deut 27:26.

9. Rom 5:18–19.

10. Rom 5:1–2, 9–10; Col 1:20–22; cf. Col 2:13–14; 1 Thess 1:10.

11. Rom 1:16–17; 3:21–26; 1 Cor 1:30; 2 Cor 5:21; Phil 3:9; see pp. 63–64.

12. Rom 1:16.

13. 1 Cor 1:17–18, 23–25; 2:1–5.

not freely give us everything else? Who could ever accuse God's chosen people? . . . Christ Jesus died for us—and, raised to life in the presence of God himself, he now intercedes for us! How, then, could anything ever separate us from the love of Christ? (Rom 8:31–35)

It is not surprising, then, that the love of Christ shown on the cross became one of the strongest forces motivating Paul's ministry:

The love of Christ is what drives us. We are convinced that if one person died for everyone else, then all of us have died. He died for us all so that we who live should no longer live for ourselves but only for the one who died and was raised to life for our sake. (2 Cor 5:14–15)

For two thousand years, the cross has been *the* symbol of the Christian faith. For believers, it has always been the ultimate expression of God's incomparable love.

JESUS'S RESURRECTION

Even before his conversion, Paul would have heard some of the strange rumors going around Jerusalem about people seeing Jesus alive after his execution. Then, when the resurrected Christ confronted him personally, he realized that Jesus was indeed alive again. Here was divine confirmation of the redeeming work that God was doing through Jesus. So the Resurrection also became a vital part of the Good News.[14]

For Paul, the death and Resurrection of Jesus are always tied together as the dual expression of God's redemptive work: "God gave Jesus to die for our sins, and he raised him to life to make us right with God" (Rom 4:25).[15] Thus, in summarizing the heart of the gospel, Paul includes both: "I passed on to you the most important things . . . namely, that Christ died for our sins . . . and that he was raised to life three days later" (1 Cor 15:3–4). The Resurrection must never be considered secondary to the cross.

Indeed, Paul claims, the Resurrection is of such crucial importance that, if it had never happened, there would be *no* Good News:

14. 1 Cor 15:4; cf. Acts 17:18, 32; 23:6; 24:21.
15. Cf. Rom 5:10.

> If Christ has not been raised, your faith means nothing, and you are still doomed in your sins. It also means that the believers in Christ who have died are forever lost. (1 Cor 15:17–18)[16]

But why is the Resurrection so important? What exactly does it accomplish? Paul makes the following points:

- The Resurrection verifies that Jesus really is the Son of God, the Messiah, the Savior, the universal Lord, and the final judge;[17] it demonstrates to the world his supremacy, power, and authority.

- The Resurrection confirms the message of salvation through Christ, the fulfillment of God's ancient promises to his people.[18]

- The Resurrection signals God's victory over the powers of evil[19] and the final enemy, death itself.[20]

- The Resurrection assures those joined to Christ by faith that they will also one day be resurrected and receive eternal glory.[21]

- The Resurrection brings new life and power into the lives of believers, enabling them to experience their own "resurrection life."[22]

The Resurrection expresses the ultimate victory of God's redeeming work in Jesus. As such, it is crucial in God's scheme of salvation; it is as strategic a part of God's redemptive work as the cross. The cross and the Resurrection always go hand in hand, and the eternal benefits flow from both.

SHARING IN JESUS'S DEATH AND RESURRECTION

When people become joined to Christ in baptism by putting their trust in him, they come to share in the experience and benefits of his death and Resurrection.[23] The act of baptism symbolizes this experience.[24] (The

---

16. Cf. 1 Cor 15:14–19.

17. Rom 1:4; 1 Cor 15:3–4; Phil 2:9–11; Acts 17:3, 31.

18. Acts 13:26, 30–39; 26:23.

19. Eph 1:20–22; Col 2:15; cf. Gal 1:4; Col 2:10; 1 Pet 3:21–22.

20. 1 Cor 15:25–26, 54–57; 2 Tim 1:10; cf. Rom 8:2, 38.

21. 1 Cor 15:20–23, 48–49, 51–53; Eph 1:13–14; Phil 3:21; 1 Thess 4:14–17; 2 Tim 2:11–12.

22. Rom 8:1–4, 9–11; Eph 2:5–6; Phil 3:10; Col 3:1–3.

23. Rom 6:4–13; Col 2:12–13.

24. The Lord's Supper also symbolizes believers' participation in his death: 1 Cor 10:16; cf. 11:27–30.

sacramental aspects of baptism will be discussed later.[25]) Going down into the water[26] symbolizes their burial: with Christ, they die to sin and the world.[27] Coming up out of the water symbolizes their resurrection: with Christ, they rise to live a new life. As Paul himself expresses it,

> Don't you know that when we were baptized into Christ Jesus, we were baptized into his death? When we were baptized, we died and were buried with him, so that, just as Christ was raised from death by the glorious power of the Father, we also might live a new life. (Rom 6:3–4)

This new life in Christ is a spiritual life centered on spiritual realities, empowered by his life within them. Raised with Christ and given "the mind-set of Christ,"[28] believers become new persons,[29] focused on heavenly things, not on things of this world:

> You have died with Christ and are now set free . . . ; why, then, do you live as if you were governed by the things of the world? . . . You have been raised to life with Christ, so set your hearts on the things of heaven, where Christ is . . . Fix your minds on the things of heaven, not on things here on earth. For you have died and your life is now hidden with Christ in God. Your real life is Christ, and when he appears, you will appear with him and share his glory. (Col 2:20—3:4)

The eyes of believers are now fixed on the resurrected Christ: he is the focus of their lives and he defines their identity. And one day, they will rise to live and rule in glory with him forever.[30]

THE POINT . . .

For Paul, the deepest significance of Jesus lies not in his earthly life and teachings (to which he rarely refers explicitly[31]) but in his death and Resurrection, the two decisive events that mark the climax of God's redemptive

---

25. See pp. 127–31.
26. For the earliest Christians, baptism was typically by immersion.
27. Gal 5:24; 6:14; Col 3:5.
28. 1 Cor 2:16.
29. 2 Cor 5:17; cf. Gal 6:15.
30. 1 Cor 15:20–23, 51–53; cf. 6:2–3.
31. 1 Cor 7:10; 9:14; 11:23–25; cf. 1 Thess 4:15.

work through him.[32] Through these two historical events, God has provided an answer to the tragic problem of sin. Through Christ's sacrificial death, our sins are forgiven—and it is the Resurrection that confirms that. The Resurrection also (1) confirms who Jesus is—the Son of God, the Messiah, the Savior, the Lord, the final judge; (2) signifies God's victory over death and the powers of evil; (3) assures believers that they too will one day be resurrected; and (4) makes it possible for believers to experience personally the transforming power of his resurrected life. The Resurrection is as central as the cross to the Christian faith.

Today, when the social dimensions of the Christian message are often emphasized, and Christianity is only taken seriously by some because of its social implications, Paul reminds us that the deepest significance of Jesus lies not simply in his teachings and the example of his life (as remarkable and important as they are) but in these two key events at the end of his life. The heart of the gospel is the message of the cross and the Resurrection—the Good News of God's forgiving grace and his victory over sin and evil. This is the message a lost and dying world *most* needs to hear.

In addition, for believers, the Christian life is to be a daily living-out of Jesus's death and Resurrection—a daily experience of dying to oneself and "rising" to live a new life.

The death and Resurrection of Christ, then, must be central in all our thinking about the Christian faith, the Christian message, and the Christian life. These two critical events lie at the heart of what historic Christianity is all about.

32. Cf. the four Gospels, all of which culminate in a detailed account of Jesus's death and Resurrection.

6

The Fundamental Problem
Sin and the Day of Judgment

SALVATION IS THE ISSUE of critical importance to Paul. But why? What is it about humans that puts them in such jeopardy, in such desperate need of being saved? And from what exactly do they need to be saved?

HUMAN SINFULNESS

With his orthodox Jewish upbringing, Paul would have grown up with the traditional belief that people are subject to both good and evil impulses and yield to one or the other. In conventional Judaism, those who yielded to good impulses and obeyed the Law of Moses were considered righteous, while those who allowed evil impulses to dominate their life were deemed evil. The presupposition was that people could choose to be and do good, if they wished.

In his early days, as an enthusiastic student of the Law of Moses, Paul had no hesitations in considering himself one of the righteous. Reflecting later on his earlier zeal, he even says, "As far as a person could be considered righteous by obeying the commandments of the Law, I was blameless" (Phil 3:6)—blameless, that is, according to the standards of Pharisaic Judaism. He certainly seems not to have been plagued by a sense of moral frustration or guilt as a young rabbinic student.

But as a result of the divine revelation he experienced on the road to Damascus and his new understanding of the cross, Paul became aware of the darker side of human nature and the universal nature of sin. He became convinced that no one can ever be considered inherently righteous in God's eyes, no matter how good his or her life, because everyone (Jew and gentile alike) falls far short of God's holy standards. Despite their having been created in the image of God, everything people do, even at their very best, is poisoned by sin. Although the details of how he arrived at this conviction remain hidden, Paul clearly came to realize that sin is endemic among human beings.[1] The young Jewish man who once prided himself on his righteousness came to acknowledge, as a Christian, not only the depths of his own sinfulness[2] but also the all-pervasive nature of human sinfulness generally.[3] In the process, he discovered texts in Scripture that confirmed this conviction:

> As the Scriptures say:
> There is no one who is righteous,
> no one who understands
> or who seeks for God.
> Everybody has turned away from God;
> they have all become useless;
> no one does what is right, not a single person. (Rom 3:10–12)[4]

How much of his thinking was shaped by his awareness of the perverse nature of his own earlier persecuting zeal in the name of righteousness (which had badly misled him regarding Christ) is difficult to say. A number of other considerations may have influenced him also:

- his new understanding of Jesus's death as a sacrifice for the world's sins, with its implication that salvation is a gift that can never be earned

- a growing awareness of God's deeper concern with the hearts and thoughts of people, not simply their actions

---

1. Rom 3:23; 5:12; Gal 3:22.

2. 1 Tim 1:15.

3. Rom 7:14–25 reflects this later Christian perspective, in contrast to the more superficial earlier Jewish perception expressed in Phil 3:6 above.

4. Rom 3:10–18 is a collection of texts culled from various Old Testament passages (Ps 5:9; 10:7; 14:1–3; 36:1; 53:1–3; 140:3; Isa 59:7–8), showing the sinfulness of all people; cf. Jer 17:9: "The heart is more deceitful than anything else—it is beyond cure."

- a deeper realization of the absolute nature of God's demands—that people must love him with *all* their heart, *all* their soul, and *all* their strength; that they must love others *as much as they love themselves*

Whatever the factors were, he certainly came to a profound realization of the innate sinfulness of all people—a more radical view of sin than anything he had known in Judaism.

When he speaks of human sinfulness, his primary focus is not on the *origin* of sin (the problem of original sin)[5] but on the universal *reality* of sin. But what is it that defines *sin* for Paul? Sin is not simply a social phenomenon, a wronging of other people. On the most fundamental level, from a traditional Jewish perspective, sin is anything that violates the will of God—that is, anything that breaks the Law of Moses. But Paul's understanding of sin runs deeper than this. When he speaks of the sin of the pagan world in Romans 1,[6] he focuses not simply on pagans' moral violations of the Law of God but on their thoroughgoing disregard for God himself. Although the whole creation attests to the reality and power of the Creator, pagans seem utterly oblivious of his reality. They have no concern for God, no sense of his authority or claims on them, no sense of the need to bow before him, no sense of the need to honor or thank him. They have substituted their own ideas for God. They are more interested in the things God has created than in God himself. They live as if God did not exist. The root of their sin is their failure to acknowledge God and take him seriously.[7]

This disregard for God is not the problem of the pagan world alone. It is everyone's problem, because no one treats God with the respect and honor that he deserves; no one—Jew or gentile—measures up to God's standards.[8] Human beings are inherently more concerned with themselves than with God—the One who made and sustains them, who has given them everything, and to whom they are infinitely indebted. The entire world is tragically alienated from God.[9]

Paul is convinced that the greatest of all human problems is the universal problem of sin, and the greatest of all human needs is the need to be saved from its terrible consequences.

---

5. Rom 5:12–21 is the primary passage that focuses on Adam as the source of sin; cf. 1 Cor 15:22, 45–49.

6. 1:18–32.

7. Rom 1:20–25.

8. Rom 3:23.

9. 2 Cor 5:18, 20.

GOD'S JUDGMENT

Behind Paul's emphasis on the world's need for salvation lies the traditional Jewish understanding of the Day of Judgment—the day when every individual will be held accountable by God. On that fateful day, according to Pharisaic understanding, people will be judged by God on the basis of their actions in this life,[10] and will be either resurrected to eternal life or doomed to eternal punishment. Their final destiny will be determined by their righteousness or lack thereof.

This is the view Paul would have been taught, growing up. It was grounded in a strong belief in the holiness of God, a belief that would only have been reinforced by his new understanding of Christ. If the Messiah himself had to die for the sins of the world, then God's hatred of sin and his judgment on it must be far greater than Paul had ever imagined.

Paul came to realize that no one is exempt from the judgment and wrath of God. Without defining the precise shape it will take, he speaks a great deal about the coming wrath of God[11] and eternal "destruction."[12] Enslaved to sin, the whole world stands doomed under his judgment, subject to his wrath.[13] Even those who seriously try to obey the Law of God fall under his judgment because of their failings,[14] for God will judge even their secret thoughts.[15] This is why the Good News is like a "deadly stench that kills" to unbelievers;[16] it brings with it the terrifying warning of God's judgment on an unbelieving world.

The threat of the Day of the Judgment is a significant part of what motivates Paul's missionary work and gives it urgency. His mind is taken up with eternal issues—the final destiny of people on the Day of Judgment and the universal need of salvation. Apart from a personal response to God's redemptive work in Christ, the world is doomed.

10. Rom 2:6; cf. 2:1–16; 14:10, 12; 2 Cor 5:10.

11. Rom 1:18; 2:5, 8; 3:5; 4:15; 5:9; 9:22; 12:19; Eph 2:3; 5:6; Col 3:6; 1 Thess 1:10; 5:9; cf. Phil 3:19.

12. Rom 9:22; Phil 3:19; 2 Thess 1:9; 2:3. "Destruction" is the opposite of eternal life.

13. Rom 3:19; cf. 1 Cor 15:17–18; Eph 2:3, 12.

14. Gal 3:10; 6:13.

15. Rom 2:16.

16. Believers, on the other hand, knowing that Christ came to spare his people the wrath of God (Rom 5:9; 1 Thess 1:10; cf. 5:9), experience the gospel as the beautiful fragrance of life: 2 Cor 2:15–16.

THE POWER OF SIN

When Paul considers the problem of sin, however, it is not only the future judgment of God that concerns him. He is troubled also by the demonic control that sin exerts over people in the present. Overpowering people and wreaking havoc in their lives, sin is an uncontrollable force for evil, as Paul himself has experienced.[17] The whole world lies under the control of sin; everyone is a helpless captive to its perverse power, in desperate need of being set free.[18]

Behind the all-enslaving power of sin lies the work of the Devil. In a passage that reminds believers of their pre-conversion state, the link in Paul's thinking between sin and the power of the Evil One is clear:

> In the past, you were spiritually dead because of your disobedi-
> ence and sins. At that time, you followed the world's evil way
> and were driven by the ruler of the spiritual powers in the un-
> seen world, the spirit who now controls those who disobey God.
> Actually, all of us were like them, living according to our sinful
> desires and doing whatever our minds and bodies wished. (Eph
> 2:1–3)

The extent to which people by nature are subject to the power of sin is most clearly expressed in the following classic passage, where Paul, using himself as an example, poignantly describes the frustration even of those who are most serious about trying to live a righteous life in obedience to the Law of Moses:

> We know that the Law is spiritual; but I am a mere mortal, en-
> slaved to sin. I don't understand why I act the way I do. I don't
> do what I would like to do; I do the things I hate . . . So I am not
> really the one doing these detestable things; it is the sin that lives
> in me. I know that there is no goodness in me (that is, in my hu-
> man nature). Even when I want to do good, I cannot. Instead of
> doing what is right, I do what is wrong—and I hate it. So if I end
> up doing what I don't want to do, it means that I am no longer
> the one doing it; it is the sin that lives in me.
> So I find that my life is driven by this reality: even though I
> want to do what is right, I always end up doing what is wrong.
> Deep within me, I want to obey the Law of God. But there is a
> different law at work in my body, fighting against my mind and
> making me a prisoner of the power of sin at work in my body.

17. Rom 7:8–13.
18. Rom 3:9; 6:14–18; Gal 3:22.

> What a miserable man I am! . . . So this is my situation: in my mind, I want to obey the Law of God; but my selfish desires keep making me sin. (Rom 7:14–25)[19]

Apart from Christ's regenerating work, people are simply incapable of living up to their ideals, no matter how determined they may be. In this broken world dominated by the Evil One, sin is a sinister force that overwhelms and masters everyone; no one is exempt from its power. The world's greatest need, then, is to be saved from its destructive consequences, both in this life and on the Day of Judgment.

THE POINT . . .

Here we see perhaps the most striking difference between Paul's view of God and the world, and ours today. As a result of Christ's revelation to him, Paul came to a more radical view of sin and the judgment of God than he had grown up with in Judaism—and a much more radical view of it than many Christians hold today. Behind it lies a more serious view of the holiness of God. Because God is the all-holy One who cannot tolerate sin, no one is truly righteous in his eyes; everyone stands under his judgment, in need of salvation. Apart from Christ, the world is doomed. Convinced of the reality of the coming Day of Judgment, Paul takes the fear of God and the lostness of the world seriously.

Today, uncomfortable with Paul's strong view of sin and the idea of God's holy wrath, many modern Christians are less certain that the world is lost and stands in danger of God's judgment. Some are inclined to believe that, when the End comes, God will unconditionally forgive and accept everyone. In general, there is much less emphasis on the fear of God and the Day of Judgment today.

Paul raises uncomfortable and deeply troubling questions for us who live in the modern world: How seriously do we take the biblical view of God? To what extent is our living and thinking shaped by the utter holiness of God, the Day of Judgment, and the wrath of God? Do we sincerely live in the fear of God?

And how seriously do we take the universal reality of sin and the lostness of the world? How do we think about those who do not believe, and how concerned are we for them?

19. For a more detailed discussion of this debated passage, see pp. 95–99.

Paul's convictions are clear and challenging: (1) of all the dire problems facing the world, the greatest is the universal problem of sin; and (2) the world's greatest need is the need to be delivered from sin—from both its eternal consequences and its all-enslaving power. So the most important question is, "What must I do to be saved?" (Acts 16:30).

7

The Divine Answer
The Good News of Salvation

THE GOOD NEWS OF salvation revealed in Christ is God's extraordinary answer—God's *comprehensive* answer—to the problem of human sin. This is the message of liberation that Paul devoted himself to proclaiming.

SAVED THROUGH CHRIST, NOT THE LAW OF MOSES

Traditionally, most ordinary Jews in Paul's day thought that the way to gain God's approval and blessing was by obeying the Law of Moses. In popular thinking, obedience to the Law defined those who were righteous in God's eyes. Even those with a greater sense of their need to rely on God's mercy would have thought it essential to obey the Law in order to remain in his grace.

As a result of his dramatic encounter with the Lord, however, Paul came to a distinctly different understanding of how people come to be accepted by God: it is only through Christ that people are made right with God. Because of the reconciling work of Jesus's death on the cross, people are now freely accepted as righteous, and it has nothing to do with obeying the Law of Moses. Salvation is simply a gift of God for all who put their faith in Christ to save them:

> Now, God's way of making us right with himself has been revealed, and it has nothing to do with the Law . . . By the gift of his grace, we are all made right with God through the saving work of Christ Jesus, whom God sent as a sacrifice for our sins. He died for us so that we might be forgiven—if we put our trust in his death. (Rom 3:21–26)

SAVED BY GOD'S GRACE

At the very heart of the Good News lies the amazing *grace* of God. The gospel is, above all, a message of grace for undeserving sinners[1]—and that is what makes it such good news:

> Praise God for his glorious grace that he poured out on us through his dearly loved Son! For by the death of Christ we have been set free—our sins have been forgiven—by his great grace! (Eph 1:6–7)

> God's mercy is so abundant and his love for us so great, that, while we were spiritually dead in our disobedience, he brought us to life with Christ . . . For it is by God's grace that you have been saved through faith. It is not the result of your own efforts but God's gift, so no one can boast about it. God himself has made us what we are. (Eph 2:4–10)[2]

Right from his conversion Paul experienced the grace of God personally in all his dealings with Jesus. Although Paul speaks of himself as the worst of all sinners because of his persecution of the Lord's people,[3] Christ showed him remarkable mercy and kindness in revealing himself to him and forgiving him.

Paul came to realize that salvation is always the result of God's sovereign initiative and grace. Just as it is only by God's grace that Christ reconciled the world to God through his death on the cross, so it is only by God's grace that anyone comes to receive his salvation personally. God, in his grace, chooses who will be saved,[4] and he alone calls individuals to himself.[5] It is wholly by his grace that anyone is forgiven, adopted into his

---

1. Rom 3:24–26; 5:2, 15–21; 6:14–15; 11:6; Col 1:6; Titus 2:11; 3:4–7.
2. Cf. Rom 5:20.
3. 1 Tim 1:15.
4. Eph 1:4, 11; 2 Tim 1:9; cf. 2 Thess 2:13; see chapter 8.
5. Rom 8:29–30.

family, and given the gift of his Spirit and all his wonderful promises for the future.[6] Of all the writers of the New Testament, Paul is the one who most strongly highlights the grace of God and makes it sing. Moreover, Paul is the one who portrays the Christian life most explicitly as an expression of gratitude for God's grace. Those who are redeemed owe everything to the grace of God.

Through Christ's revelation, Paul came to understand that the element of grace lies at the heart of God's saving work. This is the single most important theological lesson he learned through his conversion. It radically reshaped his understanding of the way God relates to people and the way people relate to him. The message of the cross is, above all, a message of God's forgiving grace.

SAVED BY FAITH, NOT BY WORKS

Although Christ has accomplished redemption for all people by his grace,[7] a personal response is still required if it is to be effective in an individual's life. Salvation is not bestowed on everyone willy-nilly. It is by hearing and believing this message of grace that people come to experience salvation individually; God's saving grace is specifically for those who put their trust in Christ to save them.[8]

When discussing salvation, Paul frequently draws a contrast between *faith* and *works* (usually a reference to fulfilling the obligations of the Law):[9]

> We know that a person is made right with God only through trusting in Jesus Christ, not by doing what the Law requires [*not by works of the Law*] . . . No one is made right with God by doing what the Law requires. (Gal 2:16)

> For it is by God's grace that you have been saved through faith. It is not the result of your own efforts [*not by works*] but God's gift, so no one can boast about it. (Eph 2:8–9)

---

6. Eph 1:3–14.

7. Rom 5:18–19; 1 Cor 15:22; 2 Cor 5:19; Eph 1:10; Col. 1:20; 1 Tim 4:10; Titus 2:11; cf. Phil 2:10–11.

8. Rom 10:17; 1 Cor 1:21; 15:2; see p. 62 n. 3.

9. Rom 3:27–28; 4:2–6; 9:12, 32; 11:6; Gal 2:16; 3:1–12; Eph 2:8–9; 2 Tim 1:9; Titus 3:5; see p. 62 n. 2.

This represents a contrast between the popular Jewish way of thinking, which linked salvation to obeying the Law of Moses (especially the laws pertaining to circumcision, the Sabbath, and kosher food[10]), and the Good News, which links salvation to trusting in Christ. These represent two fundamentally different ways of thinking about how a person is accepted by God.[11] The one thinks of God's blessing as something to be earned, the other as a gift simply to be received. Paul uses the example of Abraham to illustrate his point:

> What shall we say, then, about Abraham . . . ? What was his experience? If he was put right with God by the things he did, he would have something to boast about. But he cannot boast before God, for the Scripture says, "Abraham trusted God, and that is why God counted him as righteous." A person who works is paid wages, but wages are not considered a gift; they are something that has been earned. But those who trust not in the things they do but in God, who declares the guilty to be innocent, it is their faith that God takes into account when he makes them right with himself. This is what David meant when he spoke of how blessed the person is whom God accepts as righteous, quite apart from anything that person does:
>> Blessed are those whose wrongs are forgiven, whose sins are
>> pardoned!
>> Blessed is the person whose sins the Lord will not hold
>> against him! (Rom 4:1–8)

The citation of David's words[12] in this passage shows how closely linked the ideas of righteousness (justification) and forgiveness are in Paul's thinking. Like forgiveness, righteousness is a gift of God's grace simply to be accepted; there is nothing one can do to earn it. Righteousness is not defined by obedience to the Law of Moses.

SAVED FROM GOD'S JUDGMENT

But what exactly is salvation, as Paul understands it? What does it accomplish? First, it delivers believers from the threat of God's punishment on the Day of Judgment: "Now, there is no ultimate condemnation for those

10. These three practices served as the primary marks identifying Jews in the Greco-Roman world.
11. See pp. 61–64.
12. Ps 31:1–2.

43

who are in Christ Jesus" (Rom 8:1). Believers are saved from the wrath of God.[13] Through Christ, they are forgiven[14]—they are reconciled to God, made right with God;[15] they now have peace with God.[16]

Believers can rest assured, then, that they are safe in God's eternal care, free from the threat of his wrath on the Day of Judgment. They have received the gift of eternal life.[17] (In Judaism, those who feared God might hope for mercy on that day, but there was no guarantee or assurance of it.)

SAVED FROM THE POWER OF SIN

For Paul, however, salvation is more than a matter of being delivered from the wrath of God. As God's comprehensive way of dealing with the problem of sin, salvation also brings real power over sin and the forces of evil.

In their natural state, people are subject to all the adverse forces that dominate this world—sin,[18] the Devil,[19] evil spiritual powers,[20] and (strangely) even the Law of Moses itself, which Paul speaks of as a dictatorial force giving sin its bite.[21] Each of these destructive forces, in its own way, blinds people and brings about their ruin. And on their own, people have no effective power over them.

But when people become linked to Christ by faith, they receive new strength and freedom. Christ came to liberate people from this evil world[22] and to give them power—power to overcome sin,[23] power to resist Satan and evil spiritual forces,[24] and power over the autocratic authority of the

---

13. Rom 5:9; 1 Thess 1:10; cf. 5:9.

14. Rom 4:6–8.

15. 2 Cor 5:18–21; see pp. 62–64.

16. Rom 5:1; Eph 2:17; Col 1:20.

17. Rom 5:21; 6:22–23; Gal 6:8; 1 Tim 1:16; 6:12; Titus 1:2; 3:7; cf. 2 Thess. 2:16; 2 Tim 2:10.

18. Rom 3:9; 6:14–18; 7:8–25; Gal 3:22; cf. Col 3:7.

19. Eph 2:2; cf. 6:12; 2 Cor 4:4; 2 Tim 2:26.

20. Rom 8:38; 1 Cor 15:24; Eph 1:21; 3:10; 6:12; Col 1:16; 2:10. Nowhere does Paul spell out precisely how he understands these evil spiritual powers.

21. 1 Cor 15:56; cf. Rom 7:4–11; Gal 3:23; 5:18.

22. Gal 1:4.

23. Rom 6:6–14; 8:2–14.

24. Acts 26:18; Rom 8:38; Eph 1:21–22; 2:6; 6:10–18; Col 1:13; 2:10, 15; cf. 1 Pet 3:21–22.

Law of Moses.[25] Believers experience the salvation of Christ as liberation from all the adverse forces they are unable to overcome by themselves.

How does this liberation work? When people embrace Christ, just as they come to live in him, so he comes to live in them by his Spirit. The life and power of the resurrected Jesus himself invades their lives:

> I live—but it is no longer *I* who live; now Christ himself lives in me! (Gal 2:20)

> Now Christ himself lives in you! (Col 1:27)[26]

When the resurrected Jesus comes to live in a believer, the believer's life begins to change, for the power of Christ's Spirit overcomes the power of sin. As a result, believers can actually begin to live in a way that pleases God. By the power of the Spirit, they can be transformed, just as the Prophets predicted long ago.[27] There is no limit to the Spirit's power at work in them; God is able to do more than they can possibly imagine.[28] No longer do they need to be weighed down with the frustration and guilt of inevitable sin:

> The power of the Spirit, which brings us new life in Christ Jesus, has set us free from the power of sin and death . . . By sending his own Son . . . [God] condemned sin . . . so that the righteous demands of the Law might be lived out in us who are ruled by his Spirit and not by the dictates of our sinful desires. (Rom 8:2–4)

But this changed way of life is not inevitable; strangely, it all depends on the believer's openness to it. Although the power of God's liberating Spirit comes as a gift for those who embrace Christ, believers still bear the responsibility of yielding to the Spirit and letting this new life and power have its full effect in their lives. Becoming a Christian provides no automatic pass to a sin-free existence. (Paul's letters are full of strong words addressed to Christians living less-than-holy lives.[29]) This is why Paul encourages his readers to "work out" their salvation. God's redemptive work requires a response from them if it is to be personally effective. But even in their response, Paul acknowledges the grace of God at work:

---

25. Rom 7:4–6.
26. Cf. Rom 8:10; 2 Cor 13:5; Eph 3:17.
27. Ezek 36:25–27; cf. 11:19–20; Jer 31:31–34; Joel 2:28–29.
28. Eph 3:20.
29. See chapter 13.

> Work out your own salvation with fear and trembling; for God
> is at work in you, giving you both the desire and the capability
> to do what pleases him. (Phil 2:12–13)

This text, perhaps more than any other, reveals how intertwined God's initiative and human responsibility are in Paul's thinking. Ultimately, believers are dependent on God's grace and initiative for every aspect of his saving work—including their response to it.

The salvation that Christ brings, then, provides a comprehensive answer to the problem of sin. It delivers believers both from eternal damnation and from the everyday dominance of sin. In the words of the eighteenth-century hymn "Rock of Ages," it is the "double cure":

> Let the water and the blood,
> From thy riven side which flowed,
> Be of sin the double cure,
> Save from wrath and make me pure.

SAVED TO BECOME LIKE CHRIST

The ultimate goal of God's saving work in believers' lives is to make them to be like Christ[30]—indeed, like God himself[31]—as he prepares them for his eternal glory. To that end, God pledges to turn everything they experience (no matter how bad) into good for them:

> We know that God makes everything turn out for good for those who love him, those who are chosen according to his purpose. For those whom God has always known to be his own, he destined from the beginning to be made like his Son, so that he might be the firstborn in a family of many brothers and sisters like him. (Rom 8:28–29)

If given free rein, the Spirit of Christ works through everything believers experience to reproduce in his people the life and character of Christ. The "fruit of the Spirit" (love, joy, peace, patience, kindness, goodness, faithfulness, humility, and self-control) are the qualities of Christ himself.[32] These qualities are the evidence of God's work in his people to make them to be like his Son, as he prepares them for the full experience of his glory.

---

30. Rom 8:29; Eph 4:13, 15; cf. 1:23; 5:2; 1 Cor 11:1.
31. Eph 4:23–24; 5:1; Col 3:10.
32. Gal 5:22–23.

Paul's view of God's saving work in Christ, then, is dynamic and progressive. In addition to sparing believers the wrath of God on the Day of Judgment, God actively works to transform them, bringing them to reflect more and more of Christ's own character and the glory of God.[33] And one day, they will experience it in all its full magnificence. So Paul speaks of God's saving work in three tenses—past, present, and future: Christians are those who "were saved" (or "have been saved"),[34] those who "are being saved,"[35] and those who "will be saved."[36]

COSMIC SALVATION

The ultimate scope of God's salvation, however, is even greater. His redemptive work extends beyond the individual to the whole of creation. God's long-secret plan has been to unite the entire universe, everything in heaven and on earth, under the lordship of Christ.[37] The whole cosmos lives in anticipation of one day being freed from its slavery to decay, to share in the glorious freedom of the children of God.[38] One day, according to the New Testament, there will be "new heavens and a new earth."[39] The details of how all this will unfold, as well as the full implications, remain a mystery. (Paul mentions it only briefly.) The cosmic scope of salvation does *not* imply that everyone will be saved, as Paul's many words about the wrath of God and the eternal destruction of unbelievers on the Day of Judgment attest.[40] Nevertheless, he declares, one day—somehow—the entire universe will feel the liberating effects of his redemptive work in Jesus Christ, and Christ will be universally honored for who he is. Such is the grand scope of God's saving work in his Son.

33. 2 Cor 3:18.
34. Rom 8:24; Eph 2:5, 8; 2 Tim 1:9; Titus 3:5.
35. 1 Cor 1:18; 15:2; 2 Cor 2:15.
36. Rom 5:9–10; 1 Tim 2:15; 2 Tim 4:18.
37. Eph 1:10; Col 1:20.
38. Rom 8:20–22.
39. 2 Pet 3:13; Rev 21:1; cf. Isa 65:17; 66:22.
40. See chapters 6, 13.

Paul and His Life-Transforming Theology

WHAT ABOUT THE JEWS?

Where does all this leave Jews who don't believe in Jesus? In Romans 9–11, after giving a full exposition of God's saving work in chapters 1–8, Paul raises this troubling question. It is an agonizing question for him because it concerns the eternal destiny of his own people.[41] The Jews knew themselves to be the chosen people of God, his favored children; they were the blessed recipients of his grace, his revelation, his Law, and his promises.[42] How, then, Paul asks, are we to understand their rejection of God's Savior and his gift of salvation? Having turned their backs on Christ, they clearly now stand under the judgment of God. (Their tragic plight is seen in Paul's willingness to be damned in their place if it would save them.[43]) Has God given up on his people, gone back on his promises to them? In this theologically complex section, Paul reminds his readers of several considerations:

- God chooses who will be saved; his sovereign choice is decisive. Everything depends solely on his mercy, not on people's desires.[44]

- The Jews, driven by their stubborn, misguided devotion to the Law of Moses, bear the full responsibility for their refusal to submit to God's way of saving people through Christ. They have a long history of rejecting God's gracious invitations.[45]

- Not all Jews have rejected Christ, however; by God's grace, a small number (including Paul) have been chosen to become believers.[46]

- As a result of the Jews' rejection of Christ, salvation has now been extended to the gentiles—and will be theirs, so long as they firmly hold on to Christ.[47]

- One day, when all the chosen gentiles have come to him, God will once again turn to the Jewish people and bring about the salvation of "all Israel," as Scripture promises—presumably by their return to the Messiah. God will be faithful to his promises to their ancestors.[48]

41. Rom 9:2–3.
42. Rom 9:4–5.
43. Rom 9:1–3; cf. 10:1.
44. Rom 9:6–29; 11:1–8, 15.
45. Rom 10:3, 21.
46. Rom 11:5.
47. Rom 11:11–22.
48. Rom 11:25–29; exactly who will be included in "all Israel" is not clear.

This passage (Romans 9–11) poses several enigmas: Paul's dual emphasis on God's sovereign choice and the Jews' own responsibility for their plight;[49] his reference to God intentionally making some people stubborn;[50] and his conviction that, although unbelieving Jews are now doomed (he agonizes in prayer for their salvation[51]), one day "all Israel" will be saved. As God's firstborn, in some sense the Jews remain his special chosen people—and Paul holds out hope for their ultimate redemption. The specifics of how all this will work out, however, remain a mystery. He simply trusts that God will be faithful to his promises: "The blessings and calling of God are irrevocable" (Rom 11:29).

The section ends with Paul's frank admission that no one will ever fully understand the mind of God and his strange ways.[52] In this life, with its obscured perspectives,[53] there will always be unanswered questions.

While holding out hope for the final salvation of all Israel, elsewhere Paul completely redefines the notion of *Israel*. The *real* Israel, *God's* Israel—the real children of Abraham, the real people of God—are not simply those who are ethnically Jewish but rather those who trust in Christ and are submitted to him, gentiles as well as Jews.[54] Believing gentiles, having been "grafted into" the people of God, are now included as well.[55] The people of God are defined not ethnically,[56] but by their relation to God's Son, the Savior for all people. Paul uses the term *Israel* in two quite different senses, then—one defined ethnically and the other by faith in Christ—and we must be careful to distinguish the two.

THE POINT . . .

Set against the backdrop of the stark realities of universal sin and guilt in view of the Day of Judgment, Paul's magnificent description of God's salvation through Christ highlights the wonder of God's grace. It is the ultimate expression of God's love for a lost and dying world—*amazing grace.* This is why the message of Christ is such good news. A sheer gift for those

49. See chapter 8.
50. Rom 9:18; 11:7–8; see p. 54.
51. Rom 10:1.
52. Rom 11:33–36.
53. 1 Cor 13:12.
54. Gal 6:16; cf. 3:7, 29; 4:28–31; Rom 4:16–17.
55. Rom 11:16–24.
56. Cf. Rom 2:28–29; 9:6–8.

who put their trust in Christ to save them (it can never be earned), God's salvation provides a comprehensive answer to the greatest problem that humans face, the problem of sin. Salvation both delivers believers from God's wrath on the Day of Judgment and makes it possible for them to overcome their sinful inclinations. It provides both forgiveness of sin and power over sin.

With a diminished view of the enormity of sin and the threat of God's judgment, many Christians today are less convinced of the universal need of salvation and less convinced that Christ is the only way to God. But Paul is clear: *everyone* stands in desperate need of salvation, and salvation is exclusively for those who put their trust in Christ to save them. There is no expectation that everyone will be saved.

Paul's words also raise questions about the more limited understanding of salvation so prevalent among some Christians today, focused exclusively on justification and the forgiveness of sins. The loss of emphasis on the sanctifying work of salvation has led to a widespread acceptance of sin as a normal part of the Christian life among many believers, and left many pessimistic about ever being able to overcome their proclivity to sin. But Paul's view of salvation is all-encompassing: God's grace is intended not simply to forgive us but also to transform us. God wants to liberate us from sin in every way and ultimately make us to be like Christ himself. God's salvation in Christ provides a *comprehensive* answer to the problem of sin.

8

Who Chooses—God or Us?

WHEN IT COMES TO the experience of being saved—and of being kept saved—how much is God's work and initiative, and how much is our own responsibility? Does God choose us or do we choose him? This question has vexed students of Paul for two thousand years, and it is important to understand why.

THE PROBLEM

Many texts in Paul's letters reflect the traditional Jewish conviction that God's people are not so much those who have chosen God as those who have been chosen *by* God. Paul frequently speaks of Christians as having been *chosen* or *called*.[1] (The two terms are closely related in his writings.) Believers are the elect,[2] those whom God has predestined for himself.[3] Paul speaks of himself this way: he was chosen by God before he was ever born (like some of the ancient Prophets),[4] and he was personally

---

1. See Rom 1:6–7; 8:28–30; 9:7, 12, 24; 11:29; 1 Cor 1:2, 9, 24; 7:18–24; Gal 1:6; 5:8; Eph 4:1, 4; 1 Thess 2:12; 5:24; 2 Thess 1:11; 2:14; 1 Tim 6:12; 2 Tim 1:9. In some of these passages, *called* means "summoned."

2. Rom 8:33; 9:11; 11:5, 7, 28; 16:13; Col 3:12; 1 Thess 1:4; 2 Tim 2:10; Titus 1:1; cf. 1 Cor 1:27–28; Eph 1:4; 1 Thess 5:9.

3. Rom 8:29–30; Eph 1:5, 11.

4. Gal 1:15; cf. Isa 49:1; Jer 1:5.

appointed by God to be an apostle for Christ.[5] Statements like these reflect Paul's understanding that God takes the initiative in bringing people to himself; salvation is always the result of his sovereign work in the life of an individual or group.[6]

But in his evangelistic preaching recorded in Acts, Paul consistently emphasized the critical need for a personal response. To be saved, people must repent and trust in Christ:

> Turn away from these worthless things to the living God. (Acts 14.15)

> Trust in the Lord Jesus Christ and you will be saved. (Acts 16:31)

He put the responsibility for their salvation squarely on their own shoulders and warned them that God would hold them accountable on the Day of Judgment for the choice they made.[7] Many statements in his letters similarly emphasize that a person's salvation depends on his or her response:

> If you confess that Jesus is Lord and believe in your heart that God raised him from death, you will be saved. If you believe this in your heart and acknowledge it before others, God will accept you and save you. (Rom 10:9–10)

> No one who trusts in him will be disappointed . . . As the Scripture says, "Everyone who calls on the name of the Lord will be saved." (Rom 10:11–13)

Paul's letters include statements that affirm the role both of God's sovereign choice and of personal responsibility, when it comes to the question of salvation. Indeed, these twin strands run side by side throughout the New Testament. So who or what is it that finally decides our salvation? Is it God's choice of us, or our response to him? How do we reconcile these seemingly contradictory emphases?

For centuries, theologians have wrestled with this problem, as they have tried to formulate a way to interpret Scripture coherently and consistently. In the Protestant churches, two competing systematic theologies have emerged. Calvinism, focused on the biblical statements emphasizing God's sovereign choice, election, and predestination, highlights God's role

5. Rom 1:1; 1 Cor 1:1.
6. Gal 4:9.
7. Acts 13:39–41; 17:30–31.

and initiative in saving people.[8] Arminianism (Wesleyanism), focused on the biblical statements emphasizing personal choice and human responsibility, highlights the role of a person's response to the message of salvation.[9] The problem is that *both* emphases are found in Paul's letters.

Some scholars conclude that Paul is radically inconsistent and his thinking incoherent. They argue that the opposing statements simply cannot be reconciled logically. And from the viewpoint of strict logic, this would seem to be true, at least for some of Paul's statements.

But we must remember that Paul's background is Jewish, and the traditional Jewish way of thinking was not confined to the strict logic of the Greeks but allowed for paradox. When it comes to salvation, Paul considers it essential—as did the Pharisees generally—to emphasize the importance of *both* God's sovereign choice *and* a person's response, as contradictory as this seems.

GOD'S SOVEREIGN CHOICE

Which strand is emphasized depends on the need Paul is addressing. When addressing the faithful, his emphasis is typically on the sovereign grace of God. Every aspect of their salvation is a sheer gift of God's grace, the result of divine initiative. In his mercy, God chose them long before they were ever born, and brought them to himself. This emphasis serves to remind faithful believers that they owe God everything; they are eternally indebted to him. Predestination and election are themes intended to evoke gratitude and dedication in the hearts of Christ's faithful people. These

---

8. Traditional Calvinism (based on interpretations of John Calvin's writings) emphasizes five principles: (1) human beings are totally depraved; (2) God unconditionally chooses who will be saved; (3) Christ's sacrifice is for the elect; (4) God's grace cannot be rejected; and (5) the elect will persevere to the end (the doctrine of eternal security). The Pauline texts that are most difficult to reconcile with the idea of limited election are these: "[God our Savior] wants everyone to be saved and to come to know the truth" (1 Tim 2:4); "God has revealed his grace for the salvation of all people" (Titus 2:11).

9. Traditional Arminianism (based on interpretations of Jacobus Arminius's writings), much of it taken over by John Wesley, emphasizes five counter-principles: (1) human beings have the ability to choose what is good; (2) salvation is for *all* who believe and persevere; (3) Christ's sacrifice is for *everyone*; (4) God's grace may be refused; and (5) it is possible for Christians to fall from grace. The Pauline texts that are most difficult to reconcile with the idea of free choice are those that speak of election and predestination.

themes are for committed believers, not for unbelievers or those who are merely curious intellectually.

What about the doctrine of double predestination, the idea that from eternity God has chosen some to be saved and some to be damned? If God chooses who will be saved, does that not logically mean that he chooses who will *not* be saved? Are some chosen to be condemned? Logically, yes; but Paul doesn't pursue this logic. Only a few passages in all of his writings pose the possibility of double predestination, and they occur in Romans 9–11:

> Even before they were born, before they had done anything good or bad, God said to her, "The older child will serve the younger one." The choice was completely God's, according to his purposes; it was not based on anything they had done. As the Scripture says, "I loved Jacob but I hated Esau."[10] (Rom 9:11–13)

> So God has mercy on whomever he wishes, and he makes stubborn whomever he wishes. (Rom 9:18)[11]

> Those who were chosen found it. The rest were made stubborn. As the Scripture says, "God made their minds and hearts dull; to this very day they can neither see nor hear." (Rom 11:7–8)[12]

However, Paul's preference is clearly not to press this troublesome logic but simply to pose it as a possibility:

> *What if* God wanted to show his anger and demonstrate his power against those who were the objects of his wrath, doomed to destruction . . . ? (Rom 9:22, emphasis added)

It is very important to realize that, generally, Paul reserves predestination language for those who are *saved*, those who have responded to God's mercy; he doesn't typically apply it to unbelievers.[13]

PERSONAL CHOICE AND RESPONSIBILITY

On the other hand, when proclaiming the gospel to a more general audience or addressing the problem of professing believers who are indulging

---

10. For the original context of this quotation, see Mal 1:2–3, where *Esau* refers to the Edomites.

11. The immediate context (9:17) refers to the stubbornness of Pharaoh.

12. Cf. Rom 11:25.

13. See Hunter, *The Gospel According to St Paul*, 74–75.

in sin, his emphasis readily shifts to their own personal responsibility and liability for the choices they make. Those who don't take God and his demands seriously place themselves under his judgment.[14] Those who fail to respond to him will suffer the consequences; they bear the responsibility for the decisions they make. They cannot blame God.

The seemingly contradictory emphases on God's sovereign choice and personal responsibility stand side by side in Paul's letters.

PARADOX IN ROMANS 9–11

The paradoxical nature of Paul's thinking is perhaps most clearly seen in Romans 9–11, where he raises the difficult question of why the Jews are not saved. In this passage he gives no simple answer but considers the problem from both divine and human perspectives. In chapter 9, citing the example of the sons of Sarah and Rebecca, he argues that divine blessing has always been the result of God's sovereign choice, not human effort or desire.[15] In chapter 10, however, he highlights the Jews' own failure to respond to God's invitation. Chapter 10 reflects the language of personal choice and responsibility: "They refused to submit themselves to the righteousness of God . . . concerning Israel, he says, 'All day long I reached my hands out to people who were obstinate and refused to obey'" (Rom 10:3, 21). Note also that Paul's strong conviction of God's sovereign choice doesn't keep him from praying for the salvation of the Jews.[16]

Here opposing emphases are juxtaposed—one focused on God's initiative and work, the other on human responsibility and the consequences of personal choice. The juxtaposition reveals the complexity of Paul's view of God and his conviction that God's ways transcend human logic. This is also reflected in the responses he makes to some logical questions ("Doesn't this mean that God is unfair? . . . How can God hold anyone accountable, if he makes all the decisions?" Rom 9:14, 19). To the latter question he gives no logical answer but simply rebukes his challengers for their quickness to judge God by human standards: "Who are you to question God?" (Rom 9:20) Paul's concluding remarks at the end of Romans 9–11 are apropos:

14. 1 Cor 6:9–10; Gal 5:19–21; Eph 5:5–6; Col 3:5–6.

15. Rom 9:7–13.

16. Rom 10:1.

> How deep is the wisdom and knowledge of God! Who can ex-
> plain his decisions? Who can understand his ways? As the Scrip-
> ture says, "Who knows the mind of the Lord?" (Rom 11:33–34)

Romans 9–11, then, teaches us that we have to learn to live with paradox, and this opens up for us a more profound understanding of God and the complexity of his ways. Paul helps us to learn to live with the mysteries of God.

ANOTHER PARADOX?

Closely related to this paradox is what seems to be another: Paul's simultaneous affirmation of salvation by grace and judgment by "works." Whereas he consistently speaks of salvation as a gift of God's grace, he commonly speaks of God's judgment as something based on a person's life and choices.[17] Just as the twin emphases on God's sovereign choice and personal responsibility stand side by side, so the twin emphases on salvation by grace and judgment by works stand side by side, throughout the New Testament. And nowhere are we told how to put them together logically.

But this second seeming paradox is simply a reflection of the truth that saving faith, if authentic, will be mirrored in a person's life, in the way a person lives.[18] Real faith in Christ can never be divorced from holy living, because it is accompanied by the transforming work of the Holy Spirit; both are essential elements of a genuine experience of Christ.[19] As a familiar saying puts it, "We are saved by faith and faith alone, but saving faith is never *alone*."

On the other hand, if faith *is* alone—if the life of confessing Christians is devoid of holiness and reflects nothing of the faith they confess—then their "faith" is unlikely to be anything more than mere words. Thus, although people are never *saved* by how they live (salvation is always a gift of grace), they can be effectively *doomed* by how they live—if their lifestyle puts the lie to what they claim to believe.

17. See pp. 101–5.
18. See pp. 65–66; cf. pp. 102–3.
19. 1 Cor 6:11; 2 Thess 2:13; Titus 3:5.

CAN SALVATION EVER BE LOST?

What does Paul's dual emphasis on the sovereign choice of God and the consequences of personal choice mean practically for our understanding of eternal security? Are believers safe in God's hand forever or can they lose their salvation?

Calvinists typically argue that, just as God chooses those who will be saved, so he keeps those whom he has chosen. Believers cannot lose their salvation; it is secure. This is in line with Calvinism's emphasis on God's initiative and work in saving people. Arminians (Wesleyans), on the other hand, typically argue that, just as people can choose to embrace Christ, so they can choose to turn their back on Christ, once they have accepted him. If they choose to turn away, they will forfeit their salvation. This is in line with the Arminian emphasis on human responsibility and the consequences of personal choice.

What about Paul? What does he believe? Here again we find what seem to be opposing perspectives. In some passages, he boldly affirms God's power to keep those who have come to know him; in others, he warns of the danger of losing everything. Which strand gets emphasized depends on the need of the hour—whether he is addressing believers who are faithfully seeking to live for Christ, or those who are wavering in their faith or who have allowed sin to dominate their lives. Given the diversity of believers' responses to the Lord's claims, the presence of both emphases in Scripture is not surprising; some people need one and some, the other. Let us look at some specific texts on both sides.

THE SECURITY OF BELIEVERS

When Paul writes to encourage committed believers, he emphasizes God's faithfulness in protecting and keeping those who are faithful to him. They are safe in his care:

> He will keep you strong to the End, so that you will be blameless on the day when our Lord Jesus Christ returns. God can be trusted. (1 Cor 1:8–9)

> God is the one who began this good work in you, and I am confident he will not stop until it is complete on the day when Christ Jesus returns. (Phil 1:6)

> May God . . . keep your whole being . . . blameless until our Lord
> Jesus Christ returns. The One who chose you can be trusted; he
> will do it. (1 Thess 5:23–24)

Absolutely nothing, Paul insists, has the power to separate faithful believers from God's love for them in Christ.[20]

THE DANGER OF LOSING SALVATION

But when he addresses believers on the fringes—those whose faith is cooling or who are being threatened by other teachings—his warnings are clear: they face the real danger of losing their salvation if they don't remain faithful. Notice the following strong warnings:

> You remain connected only because you believe. So don't be
> proud—be afraid! If God didn't spare the natural branches [the
> Jews], do you think he will spare you? Look at God's goodness
> . . . how good God is to you, *if you continue in his goodness*. If
> you don't, God will cut you off too. (Rom 11:20–22, emphasis
> added)

> You will be saved by the gospel *if you hold firmly to it*. But if you
> don't, your faith will result in nothing. (1 Cor 15:2, emphasis
> added)

> Listen! I, Paul, warn you that if you allow yourselves to be circumcised, Christ will be of no use to you at all . . . If you try to be
> put right with God by obeying the Law, you will cut yourselves
> off from Christ and be excluded from God's grace. (Gal 5:2–4)

> Now he has reconciled you with himself . . . so that he might
> make you holy, blameless, and innocent before him—*if you
> continue steadfast and firmly rooted in the faith and allow nothing to take you away from the hope of the gospel*. (Col 1:22–23,
> emphasis added)

The importance of holding on to the gospel is evident also in his invocation of damnation on Jewish Christians who are undermining the faith of gentile believers by their Law-oriented perversion of the Good

---

20. Rom 8:31–39; cf. 2 Thess 3:3.

News. They deserve special punishment,[21] for God will destroy those who destroy his church.[22]

Those who turn away from the gospel are not the only ones in danger. As we shall see later, professing Christians who are living in sin are also threatened.[23] Several times Paul warns his readers that those who sin flagrantly will not inherit his eternal blessings.[24]

The seriousness of this issue is what lies behind Paul's admonition of Timothy to be resolute and tenacious in his commitment to the faith: "Fight the good fight of the faith and lay claim to the eternal life to which you were called" (1 Tim 6:12). The discipline and determination required is seen in the claim Paul makes about himself, shortly before he was to be executed:

> I have fought the fight well, I have finished the race, and I have remained strong in the faith to the end. Now there is waiting for me the crown of righteousness, which the Lord . . . will give me on that Day. (2 Tim 4:7–8)

The conclusion? The promise of God's redeeming grace and keeping power in Christ is absolutely trustworthy—but only for those who remain faithfully rooted in Christ and committed to living out their faith.

THE POINT . . .

Paul's paradoxical perspective poses a major problem for modern Christians trained in strictly rational ways of thinking. When it comes to the question "Who chooses—God or us?" we typically feel compelled to come down on one side or the other. We feel pressed to be consistent in our interpretation of the Bible. Many would find the idea of affirming both options to be contradictory and unbelievable.

Paul, however, is unequivocal: when it comes to the question of salvation, *both* God's sovereignty *and* human responsibility must be affirmed and taken seriously. Neither can be excluded if we seek to be faithful to Scripture, with its twin emphases on the divine and human dimensions of salvation. A personal response is the indispensable concomitant of God's sovereign initiative.

21. Gal 1:8–9; cf. 1 Cor 16:22.

22. 1 Cor 3:17.

23. See chapter 13.

24. 1 Cor 6:9–10; Gal 5:19–21; Eph 5:5–6; Col 3:5–6; cf. Rom 8:1–17; see pp. 102–3.

When those who accept the gospel come face to face with God on the Day of Judgment, they will have to confess that they owe him everything; their salvation is due entirely to his mercy and initiative. Those who turn away from the gospel, on the other hand, will be held personally accountable for it. Thus, those who are saved have only *God* to thank for it, while those who are not saved have only *themselves* to blame.

What about the related question of eternal security? Are believers secure forever or not? Here again we see the paradoxical intertwining of God's sovereignty and human responsibility. Without question, believers are indeed safe and secure in God's love—so long as they remain firmly in Christ, trusting in him and dedicated to him. God is faithful: he will keep and protect his faithful people. But there is no security for those who turn away from Christ and their commitment to him.

When it comes to the issue of salvation, Paul—and indeed, the entire Bible—beckons us to a larger view of God and his mysterious ways, and teaches us to live with paradox, beyond the confines of logic and the simplistic demand for strict consistency.[25] As Emerson famously remarked, "A foolish [demand for] consistency is the hobgoblin of little minds . . ."[26]

25. Cf. 2 Cor 5:7: "We live by faith, not by what we see."

26. " . . . , adored by little statesmen, philosophers, and divines. With consistency a great soul has simply nothing to do": Emerson, "Self-Reliance," 30.

9

God's Way of Making People Right

HAVING GROWN UP IN Pharisaic Judaism, with its strong emphasis on obeying the demands of God, Paul inevitably would have thought of salvation in terms of *righteousness*. What God required of a person, above all, was righteousness. But what is it that defines a truly righteous person?

THE RIGHTEOUSNESS OF THE LAW

In traditional Judaism, it was observance of the Law of Moses that defined a person as righteous. For many nominal Jews, this meant little more than keeping the laws pertaining to circumcision, Sabbath keeping, and kosher food. These were the practices that outwardly identified Jews in the Greco-Roman world.

But the level of righteousness that the young Paul strived for in his observance of the Law went well beyond that. When it came to serious dedication to the Law of Moses and the Jewish traditions, he prided himself in being scrupulous; he was near the top of his class:

> As far as a person could be considered righteous by obeying the commandments of the Law, I was blameless. (Phil 3:6)

> I was ahead of most Jews of my age in my practice of the Jewish religion, and much more devoted to the traditions of our ancestors. (Gal 1:14)

But Paul's encounter with Christ brought about a radical transformation in his understanding of righteousness. Exactly how this new
understanding came about we are not told; Paul simply speaks of it as a
revelation from Jesus Christ himself.[1]

THE RIGHTEOUSNESS THAT COMES BY FAITH

As a result of this revelation, Paul came to realize that righteousness (a
right standing with God) is achieved not by *works of the Law* (that is, by
careful observance of the Law of Moses),[2] as commonly thought, but by
faith in Christ (that is, by putting one's trust in Christ):[3]

> Now, God's way of making us right with himself has been re-
> vealed, and it has nothing to do with the Law . . . God makes us
> right with himself solely on the basis of our faith in Jesus Christ.
> (Rom 3:21–22)

---

1. Alternatively, "a revelation *about* Jesus Christ," or "a revealing of Jesus Christ
himself"; Greek *di' apokalypseōs 'Iēsou Christou* (Gal 1:11–12).

2. Greek *eks ergōn nomou*, lit. "by works of the Law" (Rom 3:20, 27–28; Gal 2:16;
3:2, 5, 10). This phrase is sometimes interpreted as a reference to certain "identity
badges" (circumcision, Sabbath keeping, kosher observance) that marked Jews exclusively as the people of God. On this interpretation, Paul is understood as defending
the inclusion of gentiles in the family of God. But Paul's argument is primarily about
how people are made right with God, not about who is in God's family; his argument
is directed not against Jewish exclusivity, but against the popular view of righteousness
as obedience to the Law. Note the contrast he draws between *believing* and *working* in
Rom 4:1–8; 9:30–32; 11:6; Eph 2:9; see nn. 3, 6 below. He argues for the full inclusion
of gentiles in the church elsewhere.

3. Greek *dia pisteōs 'Iēsou Christou*, "through faith in Jesus Christ" (Rom 3:22, 26;
Gal 2:16; 3:22; Phil 3:9; cf. Eph 3:12). The alternative translation, "through the faith [or
faithfulness] *of* Jesus Christ," preferred by some scholars (even though there is no defi-
nite article in the Greek text), focuses on Christ's own faith or faithfulness as the means
of a believer's salvation. But Paul employs this phrase to contrast two different ways of
thinking about how individuals are made right with God (*believing* and *working*; see
n. 2 above and n. 6 below); nowhere does the phrase refer unambiguously to Christ's
own faith or faithfulness. Note Paul's specific references to faith *in* Christ and faith *in*
his blood (Rom 3:25; Gal 3:26; Eph 1:15; Col 1:4; 2:5; 1 Tim 3:13; 2 Tim 3:15), and
his many references simply to faith and believing—all of which typically refer to the
faith of the believer, not the faith of Christ. Paul's use of Abraham as a prime example
of the point he is making ("Abraham trusted God, and that is why God counted him
as righteous," Rom 4:3; Gal 3:6; citing Gen 15:6) clearly suggests the phrase should be
interpreted "through faith *in* Jesus Christ." But this doesn't deny Paul's understanding
of the death of Christ as the perfect act of obedience (faithfulness) through which God
brings about salvation generally.

> We know that a person is made right with God only through
> trusting in Jesus Christ, not by doing what the Law requires . . .
> No one is made right with God by doing what the Law requires.
> (Gal 2:16)[4]

True righteousness, Paul argues, can never be achieved by sheer
determination and effort. By nature, no one is righteous in God's eyes;
everyone fails in some way: "There is no one who is righteous . . . No one
does what is right, not a single person" (Rom 3:10–12). God considers
no one righteous on the basis of his or her obedience to the Law. Human
beings are simply too flawed to live up to God's holy standards.

But now, because of Christ's sacrifice, God welcomes and considers righteous those who put their trust in the Savior he has sent. Just as
Abraham was considered righteous because he put his trust in God, so
believers are considered righteous because they put their trust in Christ.[5]

Paul draws a sharp contrast between the so-called righteousness of
the Law (the popular Jewish way of thinking about righteousness) and the
righteousness that comes by faith (the understanding of righteousness as
revealed by Christ). The latter is what he calls *the righteousness of God*, a
reference not to the holy character of God but to the righteousness God
attributes to people when they put their faith in Christ.[6] This is *God's* way
of making people righteous:

> I have given up everything else . . . so that I may get Christ and
> be found in him, not relying on my own righteousness (the kind

---

4. Cf. Acts 13:39.

5. Rom 4:1–25; see Gen 15:6 and pp. 42–43. In his earlier life as a persecutor of
Christians, Paul may have taken Phineas, grandson of Aaron, as his example—a man
who was considered righteous because of his religious violence: Ps 106:30–31; see
Num 25:1–13.

6. Greek *(hē) dikaiosynē theou,* "the righteousness of God" (Rom 1:17; 3:21–22,
26; 10:3; Phil 3:9). This phrase is sometimes interpreted as a reference to the covenant
faithfulness of God, who fulfills his ancient promises because of Christ's faithful obedience. But Paul consistently links "the righteousness of God" with "the righteousness that comes through faith," in contrast to "the righteousness of the Law." See nn.
2, 3 above. Luther's life was revolutionized by his discovery of what Paul meant by
"the righteousness of God": "Night and day I pondered until . . . I grasped the truth
that the righteousness of God is that righteousness whereby, through grace and sheer
mercy, he justifies us by faith. Thereupon I felt myself to be reborn and to have gone
through open doors into paradise. The whole of Scripture took on a new meaning, and
whereas before 'the righteousness of God' had filled me with hate, now it became to
me inexpressibly sweet in greater love. This passage of Paul [Rom 1:17] became to me
a gateway to heaven" (Stupperich, "Luther," 366; cf. Luther, *Luther's Works* 54, 193–94,
308–9).

that supposedly comes by obeying the Law) but on the righteousness that comes through trusting in Christ, the righteousness of God based on faith. (Phil 3:8–9)

Whereas most ordinary Jews thought of righteousness as something a person could earn, the gospel reveals that righteousness is a sheer gift that can never be earned.[7] Believers, then, live in humble dependence on God's promise and the gift of his grace.

What has made this gift possible? The perfect righteousness (obedience) of Christ, culminating in his death on the cross as a sacrifice for sin. This ultimate act of obedience both met God's demand for righteousness and now enables God to accept as righteous those who put their faith in the perfect sacrifice he has provided.[8] In the place of sinful people, Christ fulfilled the covenant obedience God demanded of his people. As a result, Christ himself has become their righteousness—believers are now "clothed" with his righteousness.[9] "Christ never sinned, but for our sake God made him share our sin so that, in him, we might share the righteousness of God" (2 Cor 5:21).

RIGHTEOUSNESS BY FAITH IN THE OLD TESTAMENT

Paul's new understanding of "the righteousness of God" was reinforced by his discovery of the principle of righteousness by faith in the Old Testament itself. Two key texts, one from the Law of Moses and the other from the Prophets, opened up a new understanding of the Hebrew Bible for him:

Abraham trusted God, and that is why God counted him as righteous. (Rom 4:3; Gal 3:6; citing Gen 15:6)

The person who is considered righteous by faith will live. (Rom 1:17; Gal 3:11; citing Hab 2:4)[10]

Paul came to realize that behind all of the Old Testament emphasis on obedience is an even more fundamental emphasis on *trusting* God and his promises. This is God's deepest desire for his people—that they come to

---

7. For extended comparisons of the two different understandings of righteousness, see Rom 3:21—4:25; 9:30—10:13; Gal 2:16—5:12.

8. Rom 3:24–27; 5:18–21.

9. 1 Cor 1:30; cf. Gal 3:27.

10. Alternatively, "The person who is considered righteous will live by faith."

trust him and learn to live by faith: "We live by faith, not by what we see" (2 Cor 5:7). For Paul, the emphasis on trusting God is one of the key strands unifying the old and new covenants.

LIVED-OUT RIGHTEOUSNESS

The righteousness that God credits to believers is never to be separated from real, lived-out righteousness. *Imputed* righteousness and *imparted* righteousness are inseparable twins. Thus, in several passages the word *righteousness* refers not to the imputed gift but to the holy way of life expected of believers in response.[11] Along with the gift of righteousness before God (the gift of a right standing with God), in Christ believers are given power to live righteously (the power of his Spirit), to enable them to overcome sin and begin to live a righteous life.[12] God intends his saving work both to restore their relation to himself and to change their way of life.

Significantly, although believers always stand in need of God's forgiving grace, Paul no longer thinks of them as essentially sinners and nowhere speaks of them as "sinners."[13] He speaks of them rather as *the holy people,*[14] those who have been made pure by God because of Christ's atoning work and the regenerating work of his Spirit. Their essential identity is now defined by their regenerated status.

But righteous living is not a matter of passively waiting for the power of God to change one's life. Instead, it requires a disciplined, intentional turning away from sin in all its forms. Paul's letters are full of exhortations to Christians to get rid of their old sinful ways, to refuse to allow sin to dominate their lives, and to suppress their immoral inclinations.[15] Believers are aggressively to pursue a life of holiness: "We must purify ourselves from anything that makes our body or soul dirty, and pursue a

11. Rom 6:13–22; 14:17; 2 Cor 6:7, 14; 9:10; Eph 4:23–24; 5:9; 1 Tim 6:11; 2 Tim 2:22; 3:16; cf. Eph 6:14; Phil 1:11.

12. See pp. 93–95.

13. For Paul's use of the term "sinner," see Rom 3:7; 5:8, 19; Gal 2:15, 17; 1 Tim 1:15. When he speaks of himself as "the worst sinner of all" (1 Tim 1:15), Paul is referring not to his present life as a Christian, but to his pre-conversion life as a persecutor of Christ's people.

14. Greek *hoi hagioi,* "the holy ones," one of Paul's favorite terms for believers (a designation that occurs thirty-seven times in his letters).

15. Rom 6:11–14, 19; 8:12–13; 12:2; 13:11–14; 1 Cor 6:18; 10:6–10; 2 Cor 6:17—7:1; Gal 5:24–26; Eph 4:17—5:20; Col 3:5–11; 1 Tim 4:11; 2 Tim 2:19–22; Titus 2:12; cf. "self-control" in 2:2, 5–6; cf. 1 Thess 4:3–4, 7.

completely holy way of life in the fear of God" (2 Cor 7:1).[16] The seriousness with which Paul takes holy living in his own life is reflected in his
words about beating his body into submission lest he lose the ultimate
prize.[17] Christians are to be as serious and disciplined about their way of
life as athletes preparing for a race; the stakes are eternal.[18] Even though
the life-transforming power comes from God,[19] the Christian life is still a
humanly rigorous one: it requires discipline, determination, self-denial,
and endurance.

THE SHAPE OF RIGHTEOUSNESS

What defines the shape of a righteous life, from Paul's *Christian* perspective? On the most basic level, the profile of righteousness is still set by
the moral law of the Old Testament.[20] As God's revelation, the moral Law
spells out his desires for his people, for all time. But for Paul, the entire
moral law is summed up in the great love commandment:

> If you love others, you have done everything the Law demands.
> For the commandments ("Do not commit adultery; do not
> murder anyone; do not steal; do not desire things that belong
> to others")—all these, and any others as well, are summed up
> in this one commandment: "Love others as much as you love
> yourself."[21] If you love others, you will never do them wrong. So
> if you live a life of love, you will do everything the Law demands.
> (Rom 13:8–10; cf. Gal 5:14)

Although the moral law of the Old Testament still defines the profile of the
righteous life, no longer is the believer's life governed by detailed rules but
by love. The focus has shifted from the hundreds of specific commandments in the Law (many of them negative: "You must not . . . ") to the one
magisterial, positive commandment that sums them all up. For Christians,
righteous living is understood not legalistically but as the thoroughgoing
expression of love.

16. Cf. 2 Cor 13:11; 2 Tim 2:22.
17. 1 Cor 9:27.
18. 1 Cor 9:24–27; cf. Phil 3:14; 1 Tim 4:7–8; 6:12.
19. Phil 2:12–13; see pp. 44–47, 93–95.
20. See p. 75.
21. Lev 19:18.

In his encouragement of righteous living, Paul also appeals to traditional Hellenistic virtues, especially in his lists of vices[22] and virtues.[23] (Many of these had been incorporated into the teachings of Hellenistic Judaism.) But in Paul's understanding, traditional Hellenistic virtues do not conflict with the moral teachings of the Old Testament; they are simply reflections of them.

THE DRIVING FORCE BEHIND RIGHTEOUSNESS

In traditional Judaism, the driving force behind a righteous life was the Law of Moses with its demand for obedience, reinforced by the threat of God's judgment. For Paul the Christian, however, the primary force generating righteous desires and righteous living is no longer the Law but the Spirit of God, who works inwardly to produce the qualities of Christ (especially love) in those who open their hearts to his influence.[24] This represents a fundamentally different way of thinking about how a person comes to live a good life.

THE POINT . . .

In sharp contrast to his earlier rabbinic perspective, Paul argues that none of us is inherently righteous in God's eyes; we have no righteousness of our own. As we stand before him, our only righteousness is the perfect righteousness of Christ, who died on our behalf. This is *God's* righteousness—God's *gift* of righteousness—and it is exclusively for those who accept his Son and put their trust in him. Our righteousness before God is defined not by what *we* do but by what *Christ* has done.

At the same time, God's gift of righteousness is to be lived out; we are to pursue holy living aggressively. But this can only be done by the transforming power of his Spirit, who enables us to overcome sin and fulfill his Law by living out the great love commandment. Imputed righteousness and imparted righteousness are two sides of the same coin; both are the result of God's saving work, which is intended to make us right with God and to transform our lives.

22. See Rom 1:29–31; 13:13; 1 Cor 5:9–11; 6:9–10; 2 Cor 12:20; Gal 5:19–21; Eph 4:25–32; 5:3–5; Col 3:5, 8; 1 Tim 6:4–5; 2 Tim 3:2–5; Titus 3:3.

23. See Phil 4:8–9; Col 3:12; 1 Tim 3:2–13; 6:11; 2 Tim 2:22–25; 3:10; Titus 1:6–8; 2:2–14; 3:2.

24. Rom 8:1–11; 2 Cor 3:18; Gal 5:16, 18, 22–23; see pp. 44–47, 93–95.

Some Christians today would argue that the only righteousness we ever have is our imputed righteousness—that is, an alien righteousness that is never our own, never an imparted righteousness. In part, such a conviction is the legacy of Martin Luther's interpretation of Paul, according to which a believer is always *simul iustus et peccator*[25]—justified (righteous in God's eyes) but still fully a sinner, still *essentially* a sinner. (Luther was influenced by his interpretation of Rom 7:14–25 as the expression of sin in the lives of *Christians*.[26]) But Paul doesn't speak of believers as "sinners" (as they were before their conversion); he now refers to them as "the holy people"—and they are expected to live that way. There is a world of difference between thinking of oneself as fundamentally still a sinner who may occasionally do good, and thinking of oneself as God's renewed holy person who may occasionally do wrong.

But just as it is only by grace that we are made righteous in God's eyes, so it is only by grace that we are enabled to live righteously. All our righteousness is a gift of grace ↑ *imparted?*

---

25. Luther, *Commentary on the Epistle to the Romans*, 98–99.
26. For further discussion of this debated passage, see pp. 95–99.

10

The Law of Moses Reinterpreted

THE STRONG CONTRAST PAUL draws between the traditional Jewish and Christian ways of understanding righteousness raises many questions about his view of the Law of Moses.[1] This is a hotly debated topic in Pauline studies and of critical importance for our understanding of Paul. How does Paul now think of the Law, as a *Christian*?

A CHALLENGE TO THE TRADITIONAL VIEW OF THE LAW

For serious Jews in Paul's day, the Hebrew Scriptures were of supreme importance, providing guidance for every aspect of life. The Scriptures were understood to express the nature and will of God for his people in all things. Of the three parts of Scripture (the Law, the Prophets, and the Writings), primary focus was fixed on the Law. The Law was the foundation not only of Jewish religious life but also of Jewish morality and ethics. It was the Law of Moses especially that shaped the life and thinking of serious Jews.

For devout Pharisaic students like Paul, life centered on the study and interpretation of the Law. Over the preceding centuries, Pharisees

---

1. In Paul's letters, the phrase *the Law* typically refers to the whole system of Mosaic legislation superimposed with Pharisaic legal interpretation. But sometimes it refers to the Pentateuch (as in the phrase "the Law and the Prophets") or to the ethical commandments of the Torah specifically.

had formulated several thousand detailed legal interpretations of specific commandments. Collectively, these were known as "the tradition of the elders." These legal interpretations were later codified in the Mishnah (by AD 200) and then expanded in the multivolume Palestinian and Babylonian editions of the Talmud (AD 200–600), which became the authoritative guide to the Law of Moses in rabbinic Judaism. By New Testament times, because of the multiplication of these rulings, many Pharisees had become preoccupied with the minutiae of the Law's interpretation. Jesus's sharpest criticism was directed against Pharisees who had become hypocritical, heartless legalists who were more concerned with the letter of the Law and its detailed interpretation than with the Word of God.

As a young man immersed in the study of the Law, Paul was proud of his Pharisaic heritage and achievements. But when the resurrected Christ confronted him, his Law-oriented view of life was thrown into confusion. Through that life-shattering experience, he came to several new realizations:

- Christ is not at all the person he had judged him to be, as a student of the Law.

- His persecution of Christians, motivated by zeal for the Law, was misguided.

- It is not by obeying the Law that a person is made right with God, but by embracing Jesus as Savior and Lord, trusting in him.

- God's message is not exclusively for the people of the Law but for all people.[2]

It is impossible to know precisely when Paul came to some of these realizations. How much was the direct result of his life-changing encounter with Christ[3] and how much the result of later revelation, conversation, or reflection, is uncertain. But it is clear that Paul's view of the Law changed dramatically, and this change was directly tied to his new understanding of Jesus.

THE PROBLEM

Summarizing exactly what Paul thinks about the Law of Moses is no easy task. He makes both positive and negative statements about the Law, and

2. Cf. Isa 42:6; 49:6.
3. See Acts 9:1–18; 22:6–16; 26:12–18.

they are not easily reconciled. He insists that Christ is "the end of the Law"[4] and that believers have died to the Law,[5] yet still claims that he is affirming the Law, not negating it.[6] He speaks of the "curse" of the Law,[7] yet still argues that the Law is holy and good.[8] Some scholars conclude that Paul's thinking about the Law is inconsistent and incoherent and that all attempts to reconcile such contradictory statements are simply misguided. But if we look carefully at the contexts, we find that the opposing statements are directed to different issues and are making different points.

NEGATIVE STATEMENTS ABOUT THE LAW

Negatively, Paul makes the following statements about the Law:

1. Obedience to the Law is no longer to be understood as the way to become righteous. As we have seen,[9] it is through faith in Christ as Savior that people come to be regarded as righteous by God, not through observance of the Law. Consider again these three key passages:

> Now, God's way of making us right with himself has been re-
> vealed, and it has nothing to do with the Law . . . God makes us
> right with himself solely on the basis of our faith in Jesus Christ.
> (Rom 3:21–22)

> We know that a person is made right with God only through
> trusting in Jesus Christ, not by doing what the Law requires.
> So we have put our trust in Christ Jesus, in order to be made
> right with God by our faith in Christ, not by doing what the Law
> requires. No one is made right with God by doing what the Law
> requires. (Gal 2:16)

> I have given up everything else . . . so that I may get Christ and
> be found in him, not relying on my own righteousness (the kind
> that supposedly comes by obeying the Law) but on the righ-
> teousness that comes through trusting in Christ, the righteous-
> ness of God based on faith. (Phil 3:8–9)

4. See p. 79 n. 51.
5. Rom 7:6; Gal 2:19.
6. Rom 3:31.
7. Gal 3:13.
8. Rom 7:12.
9. See pp. 62–64.

No one can be saved by obeying the Law, because no one is able to keep the Law perfectly; the power of sin is simply too great.[10] As a result, all those who seek to be righteous by obeying the Law unknowingly place themselves under the curse of the Law, the judgment decreed by the Law itself on all those who don't obey *all* of its commandments.[11] However, because Christ assumed the curse of the Law for people, those who put their trust in him are set free from the effects of the curse.[12] It is only by dying to the Law that a person can come to live by faith.[13]

2. The Law is no longer to be viewed as the comprehensive guide to daily living. For Christians, the Law no longer serves as the authority defining precisely what they must and must not do in specific situations. Believers are to be guided rather by the Holy Spirit and the principle of love, which sums up the moral law.[14]

Part of the problem of the Law is the way people come to think of obedience as mere compliance with the letter of the Law. What God wants, rather, is obedience from the heart, real devotion to the will of God. Thus, Paul argues, mere physical circumcision in itself means nothing to God.[15] What God wants is the circumcision of the *heart*, spiritual circumcision,[16] as the Law and the Prophets both teach.[17] But that comes only by the empowering work of the Holy Spirit:

> Just because you live like a Jew outwardly and are circumcised physically doesn't make you a real Jew. A real Jew is one who is a Jew on the inside, and real circumcision is something that happens deep in your heart—by the work of God's Spirit, not the written Law. (Rom 2:28–29)[18]

> It is we, not they, who have received the true circumcision—we who worship God by his Spirit and rejoice in Christ Jesus. We don't rely on external things. (Phil 3:3)

10. Rom 3:9–20; 7:14–25; 11:32; cf. Acts 13:39.
11. Gal 3:10, citing Deut 27:26.
12. Gal 3:13–14.
13. Rom 7:1–6; Gal 2:19–20.
14. Rom 7:4–6; 13:8–10; Gal 5:13–14.
15. 1 Cor 7:19; Gal 5:6; 6:15; cf. Rom 4:9–12; Eph 2:11.
16. Phil 3:3; Col 2:11.
17. Deut 10:16; 30:6; Jer 4:4.
18. Cf. 2 Cor 3:3.

> In Christ, you have been circumcised—not by a human being but by Christ himself—a circumcision that gives you power over your sinful self. (Col 2:11)

Nowhere does Paul encourage believers to observe the ritual decrees prescribed in the Law of Moses. These legalistic regulations are no longer binding on them.[19] Indeed, Paul discourages believers from thinking and living legalistically in any way.[20] Regulations like these, he argues, have no power to control sin or produce real piety.[21] The behavior of believers is ordered not by a legal code but by deeper principles, especially the principle of love.

Paul seems to consider the ritual and ceremonial commandments of the Law no longer relevant for the new multiethnic people of Christ. Believers are to be governed instead by their devotion to Christ and the transforming power of his Spirit.

3. The Law no longer has the dictatorial legal authority that makes sin compulsive.[22] Christians are free from the domineering authority of the Law that gives sin its bite.[23]

Reflecting on the limitations imposed by the Law of Moses, Paul now realizes that the Law, perversely, actually *increases* sin by stimulating wrong desires; it *inhibits* ethical living:

> If it had not been for the Law, I would not have known what sin is like. For example, I would not have known what it means to covet if the Law had not said, "Do not desire things that belong to others." Sin used this commandment to arouse in me all kinds of forbidden desires . . . As soon as I heard that commandment, sin sprang to life, and I died. The commandment that was meant to give me life brought me death. (Rom 7:7–10)[24]

The real problem, of course, is not the Law itself but sin, which uses the Law for its own perverse purposes.[25]

---

19. See Rom 14:1–23; 1 Cor 8:1–13; 10:25–27; Eph 2:15; Col 2:14.

20. Col 2:16, 20–22.

21. Col 2:23.

22. Rom 7:5–6, 14–25; 1 Cor 15:56; Gal 4:25.

23. Rom 6:14; 7:6; 8:2–4; Gal 3:23–25; 5:1, 13, 18.

24. Cf. Rom 5:20: "The Law was given in order to increase wrongdoing"; alternatively, ". . . to increase the sense of wrongdoing" (see pp. 75–76); cf. CEV: "The Law came, so that the full power of sin could be seen."

25. Rom 7:7–25.

The good news is that Christ came to free those enslaved by the Law. Those who trust in him enjoy new moral freedom as the children of God. Liberated from the chains of the Law and energized by the power of the Spirit, believers can now begin to live the kind of life the Law demands[26] (something they could never do under the Law itself). Notice again this crucial passage:

> The power of the Spirit, which brings us new life in Christ Jesus, has set us free from the power of sin and death. What the Law could never accomplish because of the weakness of human nature, God has now accomplished. By sending his own Son . . . he condemned sin . . . so that the righteous demands of the Law might be lived out in us who are ruled by his Spirit and not by the dictates of our sinful desires. (Rom 8:2–4)

Freed from the repressive demands of the Law, believers can now produce real "fruit" for God[27]—the work of his Spirit in their lives, cultivating those unimpeachable qualities that God most desires.[28] A life empowered by the Spirit takes on a quality that transcends the limitations imposed by the Law. In the words of F. F. Bruce,

> To run and work the law commands,
> Yet gives me neither feet nor hands;
> But better news the gospel brings:
> It bids me fly, and gives me wings.[29]

Summing up, then, for believers the Law (1) must no longer be viewed as the means of salvation, (2) no longer serves as the comprehensive guide to daily life, and (3) no longer bears the legal authority that makes sin compulsive.

POSITIVE STATEMENTS ABOUT THE LAW

Positively, Paul affirms the following about the Law:

---

26. Rom 8:15–16; 2 Cor 3:17; Gal 4:4–7.
27. Rom 7:4–6.
28. Gal 5:22–23.
29. Bruce, *The Letter of Paul to the Romans*, 154.

1. The Law, as sacred Scripture, is the Word of God and is still to be taken seriously. Sensitive to Jewish criticism that he is not taking Scripture seriously, Paul goes out of his way to affirm his belief in the authority of God's Law as Scripture: "The Law itself is holy, and the commandments are holy, righteous, and good" (Rom 7:12).[30] Indeed, Paul emphasizes, all Scripture (the Law, the Prophets, and the Writings) is the Word of God and is to be treated reverently: "All Scripture is inspired by God; it is useful for teaching us, reprimanding us, correcting us, and showing us how to live right" (2 Tim 3:16).[31]

2. The Law, in its moral and ethical statements, expresses the will of God for all time. Like Jesus, Paul makes an implicit distinction between the *moral* or *ethical* commandments of the Law and those primarily concerned with *ritual* or *ceremonial* issues. The moral commandments are regarded as still valid, while the ritual commandments (for example, those relating to circumcision, the Sabbath, and kosher food) are treated as having no bearing on a person's relation to God. The abiding validity of the moral commandments is reflected in all of Paul's moral and ethical instruction and in his citation of the second half of the Ten Commandments specifically.[32] For Paul, the moral commandments of the Law still define the profile of morally acceptable behavior.

But as we observed earlier,[33] his focus has now shifted from the hundreds of individual commandments of the Law to the one all-inclusive love commandment that sums up and epitomizes the moral demands of the Law: "The whole Law is summed up in this one commandment: 'Love others as much as you love yourself'" (Gal 5:14). For Paul, the magisterial love commandment is "the law of Christ."[34]

3. The deeper purpose of the Law is to make people aware of their sins and of God's judgment on them, so they will come to Christ.

> The Law says these things to stop anyone from making excuses, so the whole world will know that it stands guilty under the judgment of God. Thus, no one can be made right with God by

---

30. Cf. Acts 24:14; 28:23; Rom 3:31; 7:14, 16, 22; 1 Cor 10:11.
31. Cf. 1 Tim 4:13.
32. Rom 13:8–10.
33. See p. 66.
34. 1 Cor 9:21; Gal 6:2.

> obeying the Law. What the Law does is to make us know that we
> have sinned. (Rom 3:19–20)[35]

> What is the purpose of the Law? It was given to make us know
> that we have sinned . . .[36] The Law was in charge of us, to bring
> us to Christ, so that we might be made right with God by faith.
> (Gal 3:19–24)

Despite its promise to bring life to those who obey,[37] Paul argues, the Law
has never been able to save anyone.[38] What the Law does, by spelling out
exactly what constitutes sin,[39] is to make people aware of their sin and of
God's judgment on them for breaking the Law.[40] This is why Paul speaks
of the Law as primarily for the lawless.[41] Its deeper purpose is to condemn
people,[42] to make them aware of their need for his forgiving grace.

The Law has always served a purely secondary function in God's
scheme of salvation, Paul claims, and it was intended only to be a tem-
porary, stopgap measure until the Messiah came. It was intended to keep
people locked up as prisoners, feeling the effects of their sin, until the
Good News of salvation by faith arrived. It served the disciplinary function of a strict and unbending guardian, until people could experience the
liberating power of the gospel.[43] Indeed, Paul asserts, it was precisely to
free people from the Law that Christ came.[44]

**4. Enshrined in the Law is a fundamental principle of the gospel itself,
the principle of justification by faith.** This crucial principle, so important
to Paul, is enunciated in one key text from the Law especially: "Abraham
trusted God, and that is why God counted him as righteous" (Gen 15:6,
cited in Rom 4:3; Gal 3:6). This is the text in Paul's mind when he argues
that the gospel doesn't deny the Law but actually affirms it.[45]

---

35. Cf. Rom 5:20; 7:7–25.
36. Lit. "because of trespasses"; alternatively, "to keep sin in check."
37. Rom 7:10; cf. Ezek 20:11.
38. Gal 3:21.
39. Rom 7:7.
40. Rom 4:15.
41. 1 Tim 1:9–10.
42. 2 Cor 3:9.
43. Gal 3:17—4:7.
44. Gal 4:5.
45. Rom 3:31.

In this text from the Law itself, Paul found pivotal scriptural validation of the Good News that was revealed to him—the message that a person is saved not by keeping the Law but by trusting in the Lord. He came to realize that, on the deepest level, what God wants is not simply legal obedience but *trust*—trust in him, his character, his promises, and his saving work for the world. And that, Paul argues, is exactly what this passage from the Law itself teaches.

Summing up, then, for believers (1) the Law is still to be taken seriously as the Word of God—especially its moral demands, which express the abiding will of God; (2) the deeper purpose of the Law is to make people feel the weight of their sin and their need of God's forgiving grace; and (3) the Law affirms the fundamental gospel principle that people are saved by faith.

CHRIST AND THE LAW

Although Paul continues to regard the Law of Moses as authoritative, he no longer reads and interprets it in a traditional Pharisaic (that is, legalistic) way. He now reads and interprets all Scripture in a messianic way, in light of its fulfillment in Christ. It is what Scripture says about Christ and God's saving work through him that is most important:[46]

> God made his promises to Abraham and his "descendant." Notice, Scripture doesn't use the plural "descendants" but the singular "descendant"—that is, Christ. (Gal 3:16)

> As the Scripture says, "This is why a man leaves his father and mother and becomes joined to his wife; the two of them become like a single person." There is something mysterious about this, and I take it to refer to Christ and the church. (Eph 5:31–32)

> Ever since you were a child, you have known the Holy Scriptures, which are able to give you the wisdom that leads to salvation through faith in Christ Jesus. (2 Tim 3:15)

Just how far Paul goes in reinterpreting the Law in light of Christ is seen in his reading of one passage from Deuteronomy especially. In this passage, Moses reminds the Israelites that God's Word (the Law) is neither too difficult nor beyond their reach, so they should simply apply themselves to obeying it:

---

46. See Acts 28:23.

> The command that I am giving you today is not too difficult or beyond your reach. It is not way up in the sky, so you don't have to ask, "Who will go up and bring it down for us, so that we can hear it and obey it?" Nor is it way on the other side of the ocean, so you don't have to ask, "Who will go across the ocean and bring it to us, so that we can hear it and obey it?" No, the word is right here with you—it is on your lips and in your heart. So just obey it. (Deut 30:11–14)

But Paul sees in the Greek version of this passage a deeper reference to God's *ultimate* Word (Christ and the gospel)—in contrast to the Law—and interprets it accordingly:

> What the Scripture says about the righteousness that comes by faith is this: "You don't have to ask, 'Who will go up to heaven?'" (that is, to bring Christ down). "Nor do you have to ask, 'Who will go down into the world below?'" (that is, to bring Christ up from the dead). No, what it says is this: "The word is right here with you—it is on your lips and in your heart" (that is, the word of faith that we preach). Because if you confess that Jesus is Lord and believe in your heart that God raised him from death, you will be saved. (Rom 10:6–9)

Here, a passage from the Torah originally intended to assure people that the *Law* is not difficult is interpreted by Paul to teach that the *gospel*—in contrast to the Law—is not difficult. Paul now reads the Torah (and all Scripture) as part of the larger story of God's redeeming work in Christ. The real message of Scripture, from beginning to end, is about Christ and God's saving work through him.[47]

So whether he is preaching to unbelievers or writing to believers, Paul's focus is primarily on Christ and the Good News, not the Law of Moses. Indeed, some of his most severe warnings are directed against those inclined to believe that righteousness is still contingent on their obedience to the Law. Those who regard circumcision and observance of the Law to be essential for salvation, Paul warns, run the risk of excluding themselves from God's grace and cutting themselves off from Christ. They are relying on what they themselves do rather than on what God has done for them:

> Listen! I, Paul, tell you that if you allow yourselves to be circumcised, Christ will be of no benefit to you at all . . . If you try to make yourself right with God by obeying the Law, you cut

47. Cf. Rom 10:6–13; 1 Cor 10:1–4; Eph 4:7–10.

yourself off from Christ and exclude yourself from God's grace.
(Gal 5:2–4)

Paul's negative statements about the Law were nothing less than heretical to his Jewish contemporaries, of course. But they were troubling
to a good number of Jewish Christians too,[48] and these were sometimes
his most vocal opponents (as in Galatians). For them, the Law was not
simply the Jewish Law or the Law of Moses but the Law of *God*—sacred
Scripture to be obeyed strictly. Jewish Christians typically continued to
circumcise their children, observe the Sabbath, and obey the food rules.
Some continued to observe the Law in a more thoroughgoing way. In
the end, it was this issue—the question of the Law's continuing authority, especially for gentile believers—that most sharply divided the earliest
Christian community.[49]

As an evangelist, Paul tries to be sensitive and outwardly accommo-
dating to those with strong convictions about the Law.[50] But theologically,
he is unequivocal: Christ effectively spells the *end* (termination) of the
Law (at least as popularly understood, as a way of salvation and detailed
guide for life) for those who put their trust in him as Savior:

> Christ spells the end[51] of the Law, so that everyone who believes
> may be put right with God. (Rom 10:4)

> Christ abolished the Law with all its rules and commandments,
> so that he might bring Jews and gentiles together in a single new
> race, united in him and living in peace, reconciled to God. (Eph
> 2:15–16)

For Paul, the traditional role of the Law has been largely replaced by Christ
and the Holy Spirit.

THE POINT . . .

As a convert to Christ, Paul came to a radically different view of the Law
of Moses than that which earlier drove him to persecute Christians. Now,
he is adamant: the Law is no longer to be viewed as the means of salvation

48. Acts 21:20–24.

49. See Acts 15:1–31.

50. See 1 Cor 9:20; cf. Acts 21:26.

51. Alternatively, Greek *telos* may be translated "goal" or "fulfillment." But "end"
(termination) would seem to be a better translation, in light of the consistent contrast
Paul draws between the Law and the gospel in this passage (see Rom 10:3–11).

and the comprehensive guide for daily living, as it was in Judaism. Christians are free from the Law in this sense. Indeed, in God's strange scheme, the deeper purpose of the Law is actually to convict its followers of their disobedience and their need of Christ and the gospel. On the other hand, as sacred Scripture, the Law is still to be taken seriously as the Word of God, and its *moral* commandments are still to be understood as the will of God.

Paul has a sophisticated, nuanced view of the Law and its role. The fact that he makes both positive and negative statements about it doesn't mean he is inherently contradictory or inconsistent; the opposing emphases address different issues. Together, they express both his continuing reverence for the Law as Scripture and his interpretation of it in light of Jesus and the gospel.

Paul's words about the Law teach us that we must never think of salvation as something to be earned; it is always a gift. Nor must we think of Christianity as a way of life ordered by rules; legalism has no place in the Christian life, where the love commandment alone reigns supreme.

But Christians today who emphasize the contrast between Law and grace, who have only a negative view of the Law, would do well to note what Paul implies about the Law's positive function—the eternal validity of its *moral* demands. Paul leaves no room for a relativistic view of morality and ethics. The moral norms of the Law express God's will for all time.

From a broader Christian perspective, we must remember that the Law—indeed, the whole of Scripture—points beyond itself to the ultimate Word of God, Jesus Christ, who fulfilled the Law perfectly on our behalf, so that we might be free of the curse imposed upon all those who disobey it.

11

The Beginning of the End
Apocalyptic Eschatology

How does Paul's new understanding of salvation fit into traditional Jewish eschatology, with its apocalyptic view of the end of the world?[1]

JEWISH APOCALYPTIC

Serious Jews like Paul, living in the later days of the Second Temple era,[2] would typically have grown up with an apocalyptic worldview.[3] According to this way of thinking, which arose out of the Prophets, God would one day come in power to deliver his people, judge the world, and establish his Kingdom. Although specific expectations varied, the apocalyptic worldview was characterized by a radical dichotomy between the present evil era, dominated by sin and Satan, and the coming glorious era of salvation. The coming era would bring peace and blessing to God's faithful, suffering

---

1. The eschatological question of what awaits individuals beyond death is treated separately in chapter 16.

2. The Second Temple stood about 516 BC–AD 70.

3. The apocalyptic worldview dominated Judaism about 200 BC–AD 200, and gave birth to Jewish (and later, Christian) apocalyptic literature. In the Bible, Daniel and Revelation are commonly considered apocalyptic writings, but the apocalyptic worldview underlies the entire New Testament. The Greek word *apokalypsis* means "revelation."

people and see the establishment of God's long-awaited rule of righteousness, just as the Prophets had predicted.

However, as Jewish apocalyptic thought developed in the years immediately before the time of Christ, the new era was no longer commonly envisaged as the culmination of human history in *this* world. Rather, because evil had become so rampant, many Jews anticipated a more radical breaking of God into human history, marked by spectacular cosmic events associated with the end of the world and the Day of Judgment, culminating in the creation of new heavens and a new earth characterized by perfect righteousness. In the thinking of many, the situation had become so hopeless that God would come in vengeance to destroy the present world, then create a new cosmos. This destruction is vividly depicted in a passage from 2 Peter:

> God has commanded the present heavens and earth to be preserved until the Day of Judgment. Then they will be destroyed by fire, and all ungodly people will be destroyed . . . On that day the heavens will disappear with a roar, everything else will burn up and disintegrate, and the earth and everything in it will be seen no more.[4] Everything will be destroyed . . . On that day, the heavens will burn up and be destroyed, and everything else will be melted by the heat. But we look forward to what God has promised: new heavens and a new earth, where righteousness will be the rule. (2 Pet 3:7–13)

JESUS'S APOCALYPTIC MESSAGE

When Jesus began to preach, people were astounded by his apocalyptic message that the Kingdom of God, the climax of God's plan for history, was now here: "The time has come—the Kingdom of God is here![5] Turn to God and believe the Good News" (Mark 1:15). What Jesus proclaimed was the *beginning* of the Kingdom; the full experience of it still awaited the future.

The extraordinary things Jesus did by the power of God's Spirit—healing people, exorcizing demons, proclaiming forgiveness and the prophetic message of good news for the poor—were all dramatic marks of God's eschatological power breaking into the world in the person of the

---

4. An uncertain phrase; alternative textual readings include "will be found," "will not be found," "will be burned up."

5. Alternatively, "will soon be here"; Greek *engys*, "near."

Messiah. "The power God has given me to drive out demons by his Spirit proves that the Kingdom of God has already come to you!" declared Jesus (Matt 12:28). Those who submitted to God and his rule could begin to experience the power of his Kingdom in their own lives.

PAUL'S VIEW: THE BEGINNING OF THE END

Like Jesus, Paul preached an apocalyptic message. As a result of his unexpected confrontation by the Messiah, Paul came to understand the cross and the Resurrection as two of the cosmic events marking the end of the world and the dawning of the new era. (Pharisees typically believed that the messianic age would be initiated by the resurrection of the dead.) Believing himself to be living in the final days,[6] he is convinced that, in Jesus, the Kingdom of God has indeed come, and that the present time is God's chosen time for the climax of his plan to bring about salvation.[7] In Paul's thinking, the great events associated with the Messiah's coming (his death and Resurrection especially) mark the turning point of human history in God's eternal scheme. All the hostile powers of evil have been overcome and the Spirit of God has now come. For Paul it is a time of great excitement, with the imminent return of Christ expected to bring about the end of the world and the climax of God's redeeming work soon—the ultimate liberation and renewal eagerly awaited by the whole creation:[8]

> The coming day of salvation is nearer now than when we first believed. The night is almost gone; day is almost here. (Rom 13:11–12)

> There is not much time left . . . For this world, as it is now, will not be around much longer. (1 Cor 7:29–31)

> We are living at a time when the End is about to come. (1 Cor 10:11)

In one of his earliest letters, it even seems as if Paul expects to be alive when Christ returns at the End,[9] although that expectation subsides by the end of his life.[10]

---

6. 1 Tim 4:1; 2 Tim 3:1.
7. Gal 4:4.
8. Rom 8:19–22; see p. 47.
9. 1 Thess 4:17.
10. 2 Tim 4:6–8.

Paul and His Life-Transforming Theology

The dualistic nature of Paul's apocalyptic worldview is evident throughout his letters. The present evil era is dominated by Satan, demonic powers, and the all-enslaving power of sin.[11] The people of this world, driven by their sinful desires, are unable to live in a way that pleases God.[12] But Christ came to deliver people from this present evil age and all its destructive forces.[13] As a result, those who put their trust in Christ and submit to God's rule step into a new dimension. For them everything changes; they become new persons: "Anyone who is in Christ is a completely new person. The old things are past; everything has become new" (2 Cor 5:17).[14]

For Paul, being a new person is not just a theoretical status; the Spirit of God gives believers the means to live out this new life. Because the power of the Spirit is greater than the power of sin, those who embrace Christ can now begin to live the kind of life that God desires.[15] To the extent they allow the Spirit to be the driving force of their lives, they can begin to experience eschatological existence—resurrection life—here and now:

> When we die, we are set free from the power of sin. Since we have died with Christ, we believe that we will also live with him. (Rom 6:7–8)[16]

> If the Spirit of God, who raised Jesus from death, lives in you, the One who raised Christ from death will also give life to your mortal bodies by his Spirit in you. (Rom 8:11)[17]

> You have been raised to life with Christ. (Col 3:1)

Resurrection life is possible because the Spirit of the resurrected Christ is now at work in believers' lives.[18]

But for Paul (as for Jesus), this is just the *beginning* of the new era. The full experience of salvation lies in the future, when Christ will return

11. Eph 2:1–3.

12. Rom 1:18—3:20; 7:14–25.

13. Gal 1:4; cf. Acts 26:18; Rom 8:38–39; 1 Cor 15:24; Eph 1:20–21; 6:10–18; Col 1:16; 2:10–15.

14. Cf. Gal 6:15.

15. Rom 8:1–17; Gal 5:22–25; see pp. 44–47, 93–95.

16. This is better understood in its context as a reference to the present than to the future.

17. This is better understood in its context as a reference to the present than to the future.

18. Gal 2:20; Col 1:27.

and believers will come to share in his full glory.[19] The Christian life, then, is an *already / not yet* kind of experience: believers already experience the life and power of the Kingdom but not yet fully; that still awaits the future.

Paul's references to the Kingdom of God reflect its dual nature in his thinking: sometimes he speaks of it as the present experience of God's rule in the life of believers,[20] and sometimes as an eschatological event in the future ("his heavenly Kingdom").[21] In some passages, it is not easy to tell which is in focus.[22] Occasionally he refers to the Kingdom as "the Kingdom of Christ,"[23] which reflects the close connection between Christ and God in his understanding.

TENSIONS IN THE CHRISTIAN LIFE

Because of the paradoxical already / not yet nature of their experience of the Kingdom, believers feel the lifelong tension of living in two different eras simultaneously. Living in sinful bodies destined to die,[24] they inevitably feel the conflict between their sinful desires (reinforced by The Evil One,[25] "the god of this world"[26]) and the desires of the Spirit of God.[27] But now, in Christ, the Spirit gives them a power that transcends the influence of demonic forces and their sinful desires, so they can begin to live a truly holy life. Their experience of the Kingdom of God gives them new potential.

But in this life they will never be free of tension. Conversion doesn't immediately eliminate the problem of temptation. As long as they are in the world, right up to Christ's final victory at the End,[28] believers must guard themselves against both sin and the opposition of Satan.[29] Conversion doesn't free them from the *possibility* of sin but from the *compulsion* and *inevitability* of sin.

19. Col 3:4.
20. Rom 14:17; 1 Cor 4:20; Col 1:13.
21. 1 Cor 6:9–10; 15:50; Gal 5:21; Eph 5:5; 2 Tim 4:1, 18.
22. 1 Cor 15:24; Col 4:11; 1 Thess 2:12; 2 Thess 1:5.
23. 1 Cor 15:24–25; Eph 5:5; Col 1:13; 2 Tim 4:1.
24. Rom 6:6, 12; 7:24; 8:10–11.
25. 1 Cor 7:5.
26. 2 Cor 4:4.
27. Gal 5:17.
28. Rom 16:20.
29. Eph 6:10–18; cf. 1 Cor 7:5; 2 Cor 2:11.

The dual nature of believers' existence (the bodily life they live in this world and the spiritual life they experience simultaneously in the Kingdom) gives rise to an intriguing aspect of Paul's theology that scholars call the *indicative/imperative paradox*. The term *indicative* refers to the theological statements that express what God has already done for them in the spiritual realm (for example, "Our old self has been put to death with Christ on the cross . . . We have died with Christ," Rom 6:6–8). The term *imperative*, on the other hand, refers to the ethical demands that they live out their new life in the present world (for example, "Think of yourselves, then, as dead to the power of sin . . . Sin must no longer rule in your mortal bodies," Rom 6:11–12). Paradoxically, indicatives and imperatives lie side by side in Paul's letters.

The point is this: Although believers have been transposed into a completely different dimension and have been given the power of his Spirit, they still have to take seriously the temptations that arise from their sinful desires in this world. Although they have been effectively transferred from the realm of sin and Satan's authority to the realm of God's authority, they still live in the world. And as long as they live in the world, they will feel the pull of their sinful desires. The indicatives remind them of their new life and potential in Christ; the imperatives remind them of the need to guard against the sinful inclinations of their old life[30] and to be controlled by the Spirit.[31] What is significant, however, is the extent to which the imperatives are rooted in the indicatives. The Christian life is a response to the grace that God has shown his people in Christ, and it is by his grace that they find the power to overcome.

RESURRECTION LIFE

In Christ, believers live in joyful anticipation of the final resurrection.[32] Their eyes are fixed on that great day when Christ will return and they will experience resurrection life fully, sharing his glory and ruling with him. They know that this world is no longer their home. So Paul encourages them to focus not on the things of the world,[33] but on what lies beyond this life:

30. Rom 6:11–23.

31. Rom 8:1–17; Gal 5:16–25.

32. 1 Cor 15:51–55; 1 Thess 4:13–18.

33. Cf. Paul's indictment of Demas for falling in love with the present world: 2 Tim 4:10.

> You have been raised to life with Christ, so set your hearts on
> the things of heaven, where Christ is . . . Fix your minds on the
> things of heaven, not on things here on earth. For you have died
> and your life is now hidden with Christ in God. Your real life
> is Christ, and when he appears, you will appear with him and
> share his glory. (Col 3:1–4)[34]

Because believers are now joined to the resurrected Christ, they can
experience something of resurrection life here and now.[35] For them, the
long-awaited future has come into the present; the promises of the new
era can be experienced here and now. Each day, believers are to live the life
of heaven on earth because, for them, the End has already come—at least
in its beginnings.

THE POINT . . .

Paul's letters reveal the dualistic nature of his apocalyptic worldview and
his understanding of eschatology as a two-stage process. Apart from
Christ, people are enslaved to sin and dominated by Satan and the evil
powers at work in the world. But the moment they embrace Christ, submit
to God's rule, and receive his new life, they step into a new dimension,
the Kingdom of God. Here, by the working of his Spirit, they experience
the overcoming power of God and the new life of the Kingdom. The full
experience of the Kingdom, however, awaits the future return of Christ
and the final resurrection. Consequently, life for Christians is an already
/ not yet kind of experience. Because believers now live in the resurrected
Christ and he lives in them, they begin to experience resurrection life here
and now, even though they continue to feel the tensions and temptations
of living in this sin-dominated world. They have stepped into an entirely
new realm and—to the extent that they open their lives to its power and
influence—begin to experience the life of heaven on earth.

Recognizing the apocalyptic nature of life—if we take it seriously—
helps us to understand the omnipresence of sin, the dominant influence of
Satan, and the reality of evil in the world. It also helps us to live with the
tensions of our new life in Christ. At the same time, knowing that we have
now stepped into the Kingdom of God helps us to appreciate and appropriate all the eschatological gifts given us in Christ, including the power
over sin that now enables us to live the truly good life desired by God.

34. Cf. 2 Cor 4:16–18; Phil 3:19–20; Titus 2:11–12.
35. Rom 6:4–14; see p. 84.

No longer are we doomed to a life of failure and frustration; no longer is sin inevitable.[36] God wants us to live the life of heaven and experience its power here and now.

---

36. This does not imply, however, that Christians will attain perfection in this life; see p. 99.

12

The Crucial Role of the Spirit

THE KEY TO LIVING the Christian life, according to Paul, is to be *filled with the Spirit*. For Paul the Jew, this represents a distinctly different way of thinking about how to live a life that pleases God. It reflects the crucial role of the Holy Spirit in his theology.

OLD TESTAMENT PROMISES OF THE SPIRIT

Centuries earlier, the Prophets spoke about a future day when God would do an amazing new thing in Israel. Although his people had failed him greatly, a day would come when God would make a new covenant with them, forgiving them and freeing them from their proclivity to sin. On that day, he would pour out his Spirit on his people and give them new hearts and new desires to obey him:

> The LORD says, "The time will surely come when I will make a new covenant with the people of Israel and Judah. It will be different from the old covenant that I made with their ancestors . . . I will write my Law on their hearts and minds . . . All of them will obey me . . . I will forgive their sins and no longer remember their wrongs." (Jer 31:31–34)
>
> I am going to sprinkle clean water on you, and you will be clean and acceptable to me. I will wash away everything that makes you unclean . . . I will give you a new heart and a new way of

> thinking. I will take away your stubborn, hard heart and give you an obedient heart. I will put my Spirit in you and will make you eager to follow my laws and keep all the commands I have given you. (Ezek 36:25–27)[1]

As a minister of the new covenant of the Spirit,[2] Paul proclaims that, in Christ, that day has now come. Those who put their trust in Christ receive the gift of his promised Spirit.[3] Their bodies become a holy sanctuary,[4] and the power of the Spirit becomes active in and through them.

PAUL'S OWN EXPERIENCE OF THE SPIRIT

As Luke portrays him in Acts, Paul was very much a charismatic (Spirit-oriented) Christian. His ministry was marked by extraordinary events.[5] He received special visions and revelations from God[6] and specific guidance by the Spirit.[7] He was acutely conscious of the spirit world and depended on the Spirit of God to guide, empower, and work through him in his missionary work.

Of all the New Testament writers, it is Paul who gives us the most comprehensive description of the Spirit's work in the life of the believer and the church. Consider what he has to say about the Spirit's role in three key areas: conversion, ministry, and Christian living.

THE SPIRIT'S WORK IN CONVERSION

It is only by the Spirit of God that people can come to faith in Christ and experience conversion. Only the regenerating work of the Spirit can reveal God and make the things of God come alive to people,[8] and renew

---

1. Cf. Ezek 11:19–20; Joel 2:28–29.

2. 2 Cor 3:6.

3. Gal 3:2, 5; cf. Rom 8:9.

4. 1 Cor 6:19; 2 Cor 6:16. Because a believer's body is the sanctuary of the Spirit, great care must be taken to avoid anything that would offend the Spirit's holy presence (Eph 4:30), such as sexual immorality (1 Cor 6:15–20; 1 Thess 4:7–8).

5. Acts 13:9–11; 14:3, 8–10; 15:12; 16:18, 25–26; 19:6, 11–12; 20:9–12; 28:3–9; cf. Rom 15:18–19; 2 Cor 12:12.

6. Acts 16:9–10; cf. 2 Cor 12:1–4, 7; 1 Tim 4:1.

7. Acts 13:2; 16:6–7; 20:22–23.

8. 1 Cor 2:10–16; Eph 1:17–19; 3:5–6; Col 1:9; cf. 2 Cor 4:6.

their lives.[9] Only the Spirit of God can evoke the conviction that Jesus is Lord.[10] In his evangelistic work, then, Paul doesn't rely simply on his own intellectual or rhetorical abilities to convince people; his reliance is on the power of the Spirit.[11] He realizes that conversion is a matter not simply of having one's mind convinced but of having one's heart changed—and only the Spirit can do that.

Apart from the experience of the Spirit, a person has no relationship at all with Christ.[12] This is why Paul, according to Luke, asked the followers of John the Baptist the strange question, "Did you receive the Holy Spirit when you became believers?" (Acts 19:2).[13] The presence of the Spirit is an essential mark of God's saving work in a believer.[14] Christian conversion, then, is more than simply going through the formalities of accepting Jesus, confessing certain beliefs to be true, and being baptized. There has to be a real experience of the living God, a regeneration by his Spirit.

How do people know that God has done a real work in their hearts? The Spirit himself confirms it to them, Paul says. When believers are moved to pray to God as their Father, that in itself is the work of the Spirit, confirming that they are indeed children of God.[15] It is the Spirit who brings the experiential reality of God's love into their hearts.[16] The reality of God's presence in their lives is discerned spiritually, not just intellectually.

The Spirit also gives converts new desires, new values, new perspectives, and new spiritual sensitivity, as he works to transform their lives.[17] With the passing of time, these changes provide believers with more objective evidence of the Spirit's converting work. Moreover, tangible changes like these confirm the reality of their conversion and experience of God to others. Thus, Paul speaks of the Corinthians as having the testimony of Christ "written on [their] hearts by the Spirit of the living God," for everyone to see.[18]

9. 2 Thess 2:13; Titus 3:5–7.

10. 1 Cor 12:3.

11. 1 Cor 2:1–5; 1 Thess 1:5.

12. Rom 8:9.

13. Cf. 2 Cor 13:5: "Surely you know that Jesus Christ lives in you, don't you?"

14. 1 Cor 6:11; 2 Thess 2:13; Titus 3:5.

15. Rom 8:14–16; Gal 4:6.

16. Rom 5:5.

17. Gal 5:22–23.

18. 2 Cor 3:2–3.

The experience of the Spirit provides believers with both a foretaste and an assurance of all the blessings that await them beyond this life, when they will experience the glory of God fully.[19] Assured of the Spirit's presence with them now, they can anticipate the afterlife with confidence.[20] In the meantime, whatever their difficulties, the Spirit is present to help and sustain them,[21] praying for them in accordance with God's will for their lives.[22] The Spirit represents the life of God in them and the assurance of his blessing on them.

THE SPIRIT'S WORK IN MINISTRY

For Paul, ministry is not simply a matter of believers doing work for the Lord; ministry is a matter of the Lord doing his work through them, by the Spirit. The Spirit gives every believer special gifts and abilities, and ministry is essentially the use of those gifts in the service of Christ and his people.[23] So ministry is not the work of Christian leaders alone; it is the work of *every* Christian.[24] When Christ's people come together, the Spirit works through the God-given gifts of each person to build up the Body of Christ:

> When you come together, one person may bring a psalm, another some teaching, another a special revelation from God. Others may bring a message in tongues or an interpretation of that. Everything you do is to be for the building up of the Body. (1 Cor 14:26)

In this Spirit-ruled fellowship, believers are to let the Spirit guide them as he speaks through them to the Body.[25] They are to prize particularly those spiritual gifts that have the greatest potential to edify the Body—especially the gift of communicating specific God-given words to the fellowship (the gift of "prophecy").[26]

---

19. Rom 8:16–17, 23; 2 Cor 1:22; 5:5; Eph 1:13–14; 4:30.
20. Rom 15:13.
21. 2 Tim 1:14.
22. Rom 8:26.
23. 1 Cor 12:4–11, 28; cf. Rom 12:6–8; Eph 4:11–12.
24. See pp. 123–25.
25. 1 Cor 14:30.
26. 1 Cor 12:31; 14:1–12, 18–19.

When he talks about ministry, Paul draws a contrast between doing things in a purely natural way and doing things *in the Spirit*. Thus, he
speaks about praying in the Spirit, singing in the Spirit, and giving thanks
in the Spirit[27]—that is, in a way that is directed and empowered by the
Spirit, not in an ordinary human way. (But he also emphasizes the importance of doing things in the most helpful way, that is, in a way that can
be clearly understood by everyone.[28] Here we see again his juxtaposition
of divine and human perspectives.) When Paul speaks about the things
of God, he wants to speak words given him by the Spirit (not just by human reasoning) as he communicates spiritual truth to those who have the
Spirit. Paul's way of thinking and speaking, then, is clearly charismatic. For
him, Christian ministry, in every way, is ministry *in the Spirit*—led and
empowered by the Spirit. Ministry is the work of the Lord himself, by his
Spirit, through his people.

THE SPIRIT'S WORK IN HOLY LIVING

The Spirit's role in sanctification (his power to overcome sin and make
believers holy) is one of the most significant and distinctive aspects of the
Spirit's work in Paul's letters. The Holy Spirit is the dynamic that makes a
truly good life possible.[29] Apart from the Spirit, people have no effective
power over sin;[30] but by the power of the Spirit, their lives can be transformed.[31] They can become genuinely good people, as the Spirit works to
produce the qualities of Christ in them.[32] Ultimately, the goal of the Spirit
is to change believers to become like Christ,[33] people whose lives increasingly reflect the nature and glory of God himself.[34]

Paul draws a contrast between what he calls *the works of the flesh* and
the fruit of the Spirit.[35] "The works of the flesh" refers to the self-centered,
perverse lifestyle produced by a person's sinful desires. "The fruit of the
Spirit" refers to the Christlike characteristics produced by the Spirit. If

27. 1 Cor 14:15–16; Eph 6:18; cf. 5:18–19.
28. 1 Cor 14:13–19.
29. Rom 8:1–4.
30. Rom 7:14–25; see pp. 34–35, 37–38.
31. Rom 12:2.
32. Gal 5:22–23; cf. Rom 14:17; Phil 1:11; Col 1:8; 1 Thess 1:6; 2 Tim 1:7.
33. Rom 8:29.
34. 2 Cor 3:18.
35. Gal 5:19–23.

Christians allow the Spirit to be the driving force of their lives, their sinful desires can be subdued.[36]

Elsewhere Paul speaks of *the flesh* in quite a different sense. In some texts, the phrase *according to the flesh* refers to a purely human perspective, in contrast to God's perspective[37]—or to an ordinary human way of thinking and doing things, in contrast to God's way of thinking and doing things:

> From a human point of view [*according to the flesh*], not many of you were intellectuals or politically powerful or of high social standing. (1 Cor 1:26)

> No longer do we judge anyone from a human point of view [*according to the flesh*]. (2 Cor 5:16)

> Some people accuse us of living like the people of the world [*according to the flesh*] . . . Even though we live in the world [*in the flesh*], we don't fight the way the world does [*according to the flesh*]. We don't use the world's weapons [*fleshly weapons*] but God's powerful weapons. (2 Cor 10:2–4)

The flesh-Spirit dichotomy, then, is basic to Paul's worldview and way of thinking; it represents the contrast between a self-centered, worldly orientation to life and a God-centered, God-empowered orientation.

Paul also draws a contrast between the Law of Moses and the Holy Spirit in their effects on people. Here his view of the Law of Moses is distinctly negative: whereas the Law brings blindness, bondage, death, and ultimate condemnation,[38] the Spirit brings light, freedom, life, and eternal salvation.[39] "Where the Spirit of the Lord is present, there is freedom," declares Paul (2 Cor 3:17)—freedom from slavery to the Law, from the power of sin, and from the evil powers of this world.[40] The Law prescribes physical circumcision, but the transforming work of the Spirit effects a deeper kind of circumcision, "circumcision of the heart."[41] Ironically, now that believers are freed from the demands of the Law, they are enabled by

36. Gal 5:16–18, 24–25.

37. Cf. Rom 1:3–4: "According to the flesh, he was a descendant of David; but according to the Holy Spirit . . ."

38. Rom 3:20; 4:15; 7:5–11; 1 Cor 15:56; 2 Cor 3:6–15; Gal 2:19; 3:10, 19–24; 4:24–25; 1 Tim 1:9–10.

39. See 2 Cor 3:6–18.

40. Rom 7:6; 8:1–4; Gal 5:1, 6, 16, 18.

41. Rom 2:29; Phil 3:3.

the Spirit to live the kind of life the Law requires, something they could never do under the Law itself.[42]

For Paul, then, the key to living a holy life is to be filled with the Spirit.[43] Unlike Luke, who speaks of being "filled with the Spirit" as a recurrent event,[44] Paul speaks of it as a continuous experience; being filled with the Spirit means being directed and empowered by the Spirit at all times.[45]

THE PROBLEM OF ROMANS 7:14-25

One critical passage, to which we have already referred,[46] seems to counter the claim that the Spirit enables believers to overcome sin, and to leave the impression that they will be subject to sin all life long. The passage is controversial, and much hangs on our interpretation of it:

> We know that the Law is spiritual; but I am a mere mortal, enslaved to sin. I don't understand why I act the way I do. I don't do what I would like to do; I do the things I hate . . . So I am not really the one doing these detestable things; it is the sin that lives in me. I know that there is no goodness in me (that is, in my human nature). Even when I want to do good, I cannot. Instead of doing what is right, I do what is wrong—and I hate it. So if I end up doing what I don't want to do, it means that I am no longer the one doing it; it is the sin that lives in me.
>
> So I find that my life is driven by this reality: even though I want to do what is right, I always end up doing what is wrong. Deep within me, I want to obey the Law of God. But there is a different law at work in my body, fighting against my mind and making me a prisoner of the power of sin at work in my body. What a miserable man I am! . . . So this is my situation: in my mind, I want to obey the Law of God; but my selfish desires keep making me sin. (Rom 7:14–25)

The much-debated question is, who is the "I"? Of whom exactly is Paul speaking? On the face of it, the simplest, most obvious interpretation, given the first-person pronouns and the present-tense verbs,[47] is that Paul

---

42. Rom 8:4.

43. Eph 5:18.

44. Luke 1:41, 67; Acts 4:31.

45. The verb *be filled* (Eph 5:18) is continuous. *maybe...*

46. See pp. 37–38, 68.

47. The shift to present tense is necessitated by Paul's statement in 7:14a; the tense is then continued on naturally.

is speaking of himself and his own struggle with sin as a Christian, or (if the "I" is illustrative, as it almost certainly is) of Christians generally and their unending struggle with sin. This is the way most of the Reformers interpreted the passage, in line with Paul's reference to the lifelong conflict between the flesh and the Spirit.[48] On this assumption, readers may conclude that Paul portrays frustration and defeat as a normal and inevitable part of the Christian life.

A related interpretation understands the passage as speaking of regenerate Christians and their frustrated attempts to live the Christian life by their own will power rather than by the power of the Spirit.

However, in my judgment this passage is best interpreted as describing the experience *not* of believers but of unregenerate people who are frustrated by their inability to obey the Law of Moses fully, with Paul using himself as an example. Let me suggest three reasons why the passage is best interpreted as *not* referring to Christians:

1. It makes no mention of the Holy Spirit. The passage doesn't seem to be describing the conflict that believers feel between the flesh and the Spirit, as described in Gal 5:17,[49] but the conflict that followers of the Law feel between their sinful desires and the demands of *the Law*. Note the references to "the Law" in the passage: "We know that the Law is spiritual . . . I agree that the Law is right . . . Deep within me, I want to obey the Law of God . . . In my mind, I want to obey the Law of God" (Rom 7:14, 16, 22, 25).

In the chapters preceding this passage, Paul is responding to the anticipated objections of Jews who are sure to take issue with his claim that salvation is independent of the Law of Moses. In their thinking, the Law is the key to righteous living. With these objectors in mind, Paul here argues that, in reality, the Law of Moses has no power to make people righteous, because sinful people are unable to obey the Law wholly. In their desire to obey the Law, the frustrated people described in this passage have nothing but their own inadequate resources to draw on; Paul makes no mention of the Holy Spirit. Here, the conflict is between the flesh and *the Law*, not between the flesh and the Spirit.

48. Gal 5:17.

49. The immediate context of Gal 5:17 emphasizes the power of the Spirit to overcome sin: Gal 5:16, 18, 22–25.

2. Sin is portrayed as inevitable. To think of sin as inevitable simply doesn't sit well with Paul's understanding of the Christian life at all. (He acknowledges, of course, that sin is always possible for believers, but nowhere else does he portray it as *inevitable*.) This passage is not describing mere tensions in a person's life but utter *frustration* and *defeat*—the inevitability of sin. Note the wording carefully:

> I am a mere mortal, enslaved to sin . . . Even when I want to do good, I cannot. Instead of doing what is right, I do what is wrong—and I hate it . . . So I find that my life is driven by this reality: even though I want to do what is right, I always end up doing what is wrong. Deep within me, I want to obey the Law of God. But there is a different law at work in my body, fighting against my mind and making me a prisoner of the power of sin at work in my body . . . So this is my situation: in my mind, I want to obey the Law of God; but my selfish desires keep making me sin. (Rom 7:14, 18, 21–23, 25)

Those described here can do nothing other than fail. Defeat is inevitable because they don't have what it takes to obey; they have no moral power. They know what is good, but they cannot do it; and they know what is wrong, but they cannot avoid doing wrong. This picture of inevitable frustration and defeat does not reflect Paul's view of the Christian life generally—but it *does* reflect his view of the unconverted life.

3. The point of the larger context (both before and after this passage) is that God has now given believers a power to overcome sin. Notice carefully Paul's strong assertions in the sections immediately preceding this passage:

> We know that our old self has been put to death with Christ on the cross, so that our sinful bodies should no longer be the slaves of sin. For when we die, we are set free from the power of sin. Since we have died with Christ, we believe that we will also live with him . . . Think of yourselves, then, as dead to the power of sin but alive to God in Christ Jesus. Sin must no longer rule in your mortal bodies . . . Nor must you surrender any part of yourselves to sin . . . Instead, give yourselves to God, as those who have been raised from death to life, and surrender your whole being to him . . . Sin must not be your master. (Rom 6:6–14)

> You used to be slaves of sin, but now you have obeyed with all your heart the teaching you received. Now you are set free from sin and have become slaves of righteousness . . . Now you must surrender yourselves entirely to be slaves of righteousness . . . Now you have been set free from sin and are the slaves of God. (Rom 6:17–22)

> When we lived in sin, the Law stirred up sinful desires in our bodies and doomed us to die. Now, however, we are free from the Law; we have died to it, so we are no longer its prisoners. No longer do we serve God in the old way, by obeying the written Law; now we serve in the new way, by obeying his Spirit. (Rom 7:5–6)

Even more significant, note Paul's emphasis on the power of the Spirit over sin in the section immediately following this passage:

> The power of the Spirit, which brings us new life in Christ Jesus, has set us free from the power of sin and death. What the Law could never accomplish because of the weakness of human nature, God has now accomplished. By sending his own Son . . . he condemned sin . . . so that the righteous demands of the Law might be lived out in us who are ruled by his Spirit and not by the dictates of our sinful desires . . . If you let your life be dominated by your sinful desires, you are going to die; but if by the Spirit you say no to the sinful actions of your body, you will live. It is those who are led by God's Spirit who are the children of God. (Rom 8:2–17)

In the passages both preceding and following Rom 7:14–25, then, Paul is making the point that, in Jesus Christ, believers have been given power to overcome sin.

The frustration and defeat expressed in Rom 7:14–25 is best interpreted, therefore, as describing the experience not of Christians, but of those who want to obey the Law fully but cannot because they lack the power of God's Spirit. What Paul is emphasizing in Rom 7:14–25, then— to Jews arguing that obedience to the Law is essential if a person is to be considered righteous by God—is the fundamental inability of people, on their own, to fulfill the moral demands of the Law. The real key to righteous living, Paul insists, lies not in the Law of Moses but in the life-transforming power of the Spirit of God, which comes from Christ.[50]

---

50. Rom 8:1–4, 9–14; Gal 5:16, 18, 22–25.

Much hangs on our interpretation of this key passage. (That is why I have discussed it at length.) Those who interpret it as the experience of believers may pessimistically conclude that they are doomed to experience nothing but failure all life long—that sin is inevitable. But those who interpret the passage as part of Paul's extended argument against a salvific understanding of the Law of Moses, and read it in light of his consistent emphasis on the power of the Spirit over sin, will appreciate his more optimistic view of the Christian life in the larger context. No longer is sin inevitable, because believers can now overcome sin by the Spirit of the resurrected Christ within them.

Note, however, that this does not deny the continuing problems that Christians have with temptation and sin. All life long, Paul cautions, Christians will feel tensions between their sinful desires and God's desires for them. They may fail many times. (Paul does not imply that Christians will ever attain perfection in this life.) Only to the extent that they allow the Spirit to control their lives will they be able to overcome the power of sin and live a life pleasing to God.

THE POINT . . .

For Paul, the Holy Spirit plays a pivotal role in virtually every aspect of becoming and being a Christian. Apart from the regenerating work of the Spirit, a person has no relation with Christ at all. The Spirit is the active force in bringing people to faith in Christ. The Spirit is also the crucial factor in Christian ministry, which is essentially the use of the Spirit's gifts in the service of Christ and his people. And the Spirit is the key to holy living and to becoming all that God wants a person to be. By the power of the Spirit, believers overcome sin and become more like Christ. For Paul, the whole of the Christian life is rooted in and dependent on the work of God's Spirit.

Christians vary considerably in their understanding of the Holy Spirit and his role in the Christian community today. Some (from Pentecostal traditions especially) give the work of the Spirit such a central role (both in the church and in the life of the individual believer) that it overshadows the work of God the Father and Christ the Savior. (For Paul, the Spirit's work is always *in the service of* God the Father and the Lord Jesus Christ.) For others (from more strictly rational traditions), the work of the Spirit is hidden in the shadow of the other two members of the Trinity.

With his charismatic perspective and thoroughgoing reliance on the Spirit, Paul challenges our rationalistic Western approach to the Christian faith. He teaches us that life is essentially *spiritual, not simply rational*.[51] In everything, we are dependent on *God's* work, *God's* wisdom, *God's* guidance, and *God's* power, more than our own; in everything we are dependent on the work and power of his Spirit. Every part of our life is to be transformed by his Spirit. The key to fruitful Christian life and ministry, then, is to be filled with the Spirit.[52] In every way, the Christian life is life *in the Spirit*.

---

51. Cf. John 4:24: "God is essentially Spirit, and those who worship him must worship in Spirit and in truth."

52. Eph 5:18.

13

What if Christians Continue in Sin?

WHAT IF PATTERNS OF sin persist in a Christian's life? What if people say they are simply unable to overcome sin? (Some Christians feel continually defeated by sin.) What if a professing believer's life fails to reflect God's saving work? Does it mean the person is not truly saved? How much room (if any) does Paul allow for sin in a believer's life?

As troubling as they are, these are important questions to ask. For a continuing pattern of sin inevitably raises questions about the reality of a person's experience of God. At the same time, the difficulty of assessing the authenticity of anyone's confessed relationship to God must readily be acknowledged; God alone knows the heart.

LIMITS TO GRACE?

In Paul's thinking generally, the seriousness of the problem seems to depend on just how great the dichotomy is between the faith a person professes and the lifestyle he or she lives.

On the one hand, Paul clearly recognizes that there are numbers of believers who stand in need of serious moral exhortation. The sheer volume of admonition in his letters says as much. He is obviously aware that some of his converts live with serious failings, though he is never content for them to remain that way. The behavior of some Corinthian believers, for example, is far from ideal (Paul speaks of them as "immature and worldly, not spiritual"), but he still regards them as authentic Christians (he calls them "babies in Christ"[1]), not unbelievers. In this case, their failings don't deny the reality of their forgiven status and the validity of their relationship to Christ; they are under the grace of God.

On the other hand, in cases of more extreme contradiction—when the lives of professing Christians are distinctly out of keeping with the will of God and utterly at odds with the faith they profess, when sin is clearly the dominant driving force of their lives—then, without apology and in the most straightforward way, Paul warns his readers that such people will have no part in the Kingdom of God. Such a lifestyle effectively puts the lie to any confession of faith.

A person's life *must* reflect something of the person's confession of faith, then, if the faith is to be considered genuine. As James emphasizes, "Faith that is not lived out is dead" (James 2:26).

Consider the following strong warnings of Paul, all of which are addressed to professing believers:

> Those whose minds are controlled by their sinful desires will die . . . If your life is controlled by your sinful desires, you are going to die. (Rom 8:6, 13)

> Remember, evil people will have no part in the Kingdom of God. Don't fool yourselves: no one who is immoral, or who worships idols, or who is unfaithful in marriage, or who is a pervert or practices homosexuality, will ever have any part in God's Kingdom. Nor will anyone who is a compulsive thief or greedy, or an alcoholic, or anyone who badmouths and cheats others. (1 Cor 6:9–10)

> When people give in to their sinful desires, they do all kinds of immoral, filthy, and shameful things. They worship idols and engage in witchcraft. They hate others and they fight. They become jealous, angry, and selfish. They argue and become divisive and envious. They get drunk, carouse at wild parties, and do other things like these. I warned you before, and I warn you again: people who live like this will have no part in the Kingdom of God. (Gal 5:19–21)

> You may be sure of this, that no one who is immoral, or whose life is filthy or greedy (which is another form of idolatry), will ever have any part in the Kingdom of Christ and of God. (Eph 5:5)

1. 1 Cor 3:1

> So put to death your sinful earthly desires—sexual immorality,
> filthy lust, and evil passions. And don't be greedy—that is an-
> other form of idolatry. The wrath of God is coming on people
> who do these things. (Col 3:5–6)

Those who live an openly sinful life, Paul warns, will be considered unbelievers and will suffer the brunt of God's anger on the Day of Judgment.
Such a lifestyle is simply incompatible with a true confession of faith
in Christ, who came to save his people from sin. Real believers take sin
seriously.

Paul doesn't mince words when addressing Christians who are
tempted to sin. As baptized believers, they must give heed to the terrible
judgment that God poured out on his "baptized" people under the old
covenant, when many, living effectively as unbelievers, died in the desert
because of their sin.[2]

Christians must remember that how they live reveals who their real
master is:

> Surely you know that when you surrender yourselves as slaves
> to obey someone, you are in fact slaves of the master you obey—
> whether it is sin, which results in death, or obedience, which
> results in righteousness. (Rom 6:16)

If sin clearly dominates the life of confessing believers, it shows that their
real master is not Christ but sin. They cannot fool God: they will always
harvest what they plant—and those who plant in the field of their sinful
desires will ultimately harvest death.[3] Even Paul himself subjects his body
to a strict regimen of discipline to keep from being disqualified from the
eternal reward.[4] Believers must take extreme care, then, to avoid doing
anything that would either destroy themselves or cause the ruin of other
believers by encouraging them to violate their conscience.[5] In cases such
as these, Paul's strong words about God's judgment seem to imply the possible loss of salvation.

But it is important to note that warnings like these are typically directed against those who have *willfully* chosen to live in a way that violates
the will of God (compare the sentence of death for *deliberate* sin in the

---

2. 1 Cor 10:1–11, referring to various passages in Exodus and Numbers.

3. Gal 6:7–8; cf. Rom 8:13.

4. 1 Cor 9:24–27.

5. Rom 14:13–15, 20–23; 1 Cor 8:9–13.

Old Testament[6])—not sincere believers who are grieved by the pain their failings cause God. Repentant Christians who sincerely regret their sins may take comfort in the following affirmations of Paul:

- God's forgiving grace is greater than all their sins and failings.[7]

- Christ himself intercedes for them, just as his Spirit does within them.[8]

- Nothing in all creation has the power to alienate them from God's love for them in Christ.[9]

Those with sensitive consciences who regret their sins and repent can rest assured in God's forgiving grace; their heavenly Father is on their side.

REDEEMED BUT STILL ACCOUNTABLE

In other cases, Paul speaks of God's judgment on sinning believers in less severe, more disciplinary ways. In these cases, the goal of God's chastisement is their restoration. For example, those in Corinth who fail to take the Lord's Supper seriously suffer physical weakness, sickness, or (in some cases) death because of it; but God's purpose in this is to correct them and protect them from ultimate condemnation.[10] Even the Corinthian man whose inordinate immorality merits expulsion from the church and the punishment of Satan is to be disciplined in the hope that his spirit may ultimately be saved.[11]

Although sincere believers are exempt from the threat of condemnation on the Day of Judgment,[12] they will still be held accountable for how they have lived. On that Day, believers will face their own kind of judgment, with the possible risk of losing some unspecified reward:

> All of us will stand before God, to be judged by him . . . Each of us will have to give an account to God for what we have done. (Rom 14:10, 12)

6. Num 15:30–31.
7. Rom 5:12–21.
8. Rom 8:26–27, 34.
9. Rom 8:31–39.
10. 1 Cor 11:29–32.
11. 1 Cor 5:1–5.
12. Rom 8:1.

> Whatever we build on that foundation [Christ] will be tested by fire on the Day of Judgment. If what was built survives the fire, we will be rewarded. But if it is burnt up, we will lose out. Yet we ourselves will be saved—but only like someone escaping from the flames. (1 Cor 3:13–15)

> Christ will judge each one of us for the good or bad we do while living in these bodies. (2 Cor 5:10)[13]

Although many questions remain unanswered, it is clear that assured believers must live soberly and reverently before God, with "fear and trembling"[14] in light of his judgment. They must always be vigilant: "If you think you are standing firm, be careful you don't fall" (1 Cor 10:12). Paul's desire is that his converts live in such a way that the Lord will find them pure and blameless on the day of his return.[15] This desire itself reflects his conviction that those who are secure in Christ will be held accountable on the Day of Judgment for how they have lived, like everyone else.

THE POINT . . .

Paul's letters are unambiguous: sin must never be taken lightly—must never simply be accepted—either in an individual believer's life or in the church. Sin must always be taken seriously. Although sincere believers are exempt from the threat of ultimate condemnation and secure in God's care, yielding to sin may render them liable to some form of judgment. In extreme cases, turning from Christ or giving oneself to unholy living may even exclude a person from the Kingdom of God; such actions represent a thoroughgoing denial of one's supposed faith in Christ as Lord. So the consequences of sin can be severe—and in some cases at least, fatal.

Paul's words provide a serious challenge to Christians whose theology exempts believers from any form of God's judgment. Many Protestants, relying on God's forgiving grace, place little emphasis on any future accountability for believers and give little thought to living in the fear of God. Some would even judge that an inappropriate way of thinking for those who are now forgiven. Because of this attitude, sin easily comes to be taken lightly.

---

13. Cf. Col 3:25.
14. Phil 2:12; cf. 2 Cor 5:11; 7:1.
15. Phil 1:9–10; 1 Thess 3:12–13; 5:23; cf. 1 Cor 1:8.

As Christians, we are all dependent on God's mercy and his promises of grace. These promises give powerful reassurance to Christians who sincerely turn to him in repentance for their sins.[16] But Paul offers *no* reassuring words for those who willfully continue in sin without regret—only words of judgment.

As God's holy people, we are to resist all sinful tendencies and to live in reverential fear, even as his redeemed people.

16. Cf. 1 John 1:9: "If we confess our sins to God, he can always be trusted to forgive us and make us clean."

14

What Motivates Christian Living?

WHAT MOTIVATES CHRISTIAN LIVING?[1] To what does Paul appeal, to encourage believers to live in a Christian way? Are some motives more appropriate or more effective than others? Are Christians motivated by different considerations than devout Jews are? Do motives even matter, so long as people do the right thing?

MOTIVATION IN JUDAISM

Growing up as an orthodox Jew, Paul would have claimed to take seriously the fear of God. Most Jews had at least a nominal respect for the Almighty and the threat of his judgment. Judging from rabbinic literature, it was the fear of God (even if half-hearted), as much as anything, that motivated *old perspective!* ordinary Jews to comply with the Law of Moses. Everyone knew the fundamental principle of the Torah: obedience brings blessing, but disobedience brings punishment.[2]

In some Old Testament passages, fearing God and loving God sit side by side, without any sense of contradiction: "Now, Israel, what does the Lord your God require of you? Simply to fear the Lord your God, to walk in all his ways, to love him . . . " (Deut 10:12). Some rabbis, however, suspicious of the link between fear and self-interest, insisted that

---

1. This chapter reflects ideas found in Mohrlang, *Matthew and Paul.*
2. Deut 27:11—28:68.

obedience motivated by love for God was intrinsically better than obedience motivated by the fear of God. In the words of Rabbi Simeon ben Eleazar, "Greater is he who acts from love than he who acts from fear."[3] Nevertheless, even Jews who attempted to live a life of love for God may have been influenced by the fact that love is *commanded* in Scripture,[4] and commandments carry with them the implicit threat of sanctions.

How sophisticated Paul's understanding of motivation was in his days as a rabbinic student is impossible to assess. As a Christian, however, he clearly came to think deeply about the motivation of behavior in light of Jesus and the gospel. He knows that when people become joined to Christ, their desires, values, priorities, and perspectives on life change, enabling them to be governed by quite different considerations than those that govern unbelievers. He also knows that the commandments of the Law, the traditional force driving the pursuit of righteousness in Judaism, have no power in themselves to effect the kind of truly good life that pleases God, given the perverse, all-infecting nature of human sin.[5]

So what is it that motivates Christian living, in Paul's thinking?

GOD'S GRACE IN CHRIST

One of the most striking aspects of Paul's exhortation is the extent to which he roots it in the believer's relationship to Christ and the gospel. (Note how frequently the phrases "in Christ," "in the Lord," "with Christ," and "through Christ" occur in his ethical commands.[6])

For Paul, Christian living is motivated, above all, by the love of God revealed in Christ—the incomparable greatness of God's grace and the implicit claim it makes on a believer's life. It is the obligation not of law but of grace. For Paul, the Christian life is an expression of gratitude for God's goodness, a way of saying "Thank you."

Three of his letters (Romans, Ephesians, and Colossians) illustrate this point nicely. Each of these letters is broken into two major sections: (1) a section emphasizing God's redeeming grace in Christ and (2) a section on the transformed life Christians are to live in response,[7] introduced

3. *b. B. Bat. Sotah* 31a.
4. Deut 6:4–5; Lev 19:18.
5. Rom 1:18—3:20; 7:14–25; see pp. 71–72, 95–99.
6. See Campbell, *Paul and Union with Christ.*
7. Galatians, though primarily about salvation, reflects the same two-part structure: 1:1— 5:12 / 5:13—6:18.

by the word *therefore* or *so* (referring to the preceding emphasis on God's grace):

> So I urge you, brothers and sisters, because of the mercies of God, to dedicate your lives to him, as a kind of living sacrifice. (Rom 12:1)

> So I urge you . . . to live in a way that is worthy of being the chosen people of God. (Eph 4:1)

> So put to death your sinful earthly desires. (Col 3:5)

The Christian life is to be a joyful expression of thanksgiving for God's grace in Christ and the personal gift of salvation. This is why the terms *joy*,[8] *rejoice*,[9] *thanksgiving*,[10] and *give thanks*[11] occur so frequently in Paul's words about the Christian life; joy and thanksgiving are simply fitting responses to God's gift of grace.[12]

This joyful expression of gratitude is closely related to Paul's emphasis on living for the praise[13] and glory[14] of God: "Whether you eat or drink—or whatever you do—do it all for the glory of God" (1 Cor 10:31). As those who owe God everything, knowing that it is only by his grace that they are saved, believers are to give praise to God in everything they do. Living for the glory of God is part of what Paul means when he speaks of living in a way that is "worthy" of the Lord and the gospel.[15] God's life-saving grace deserves nothing less than wholehearted dedication to living for him.[16]

8. Rom 14:17; 15:13; 2 Cor 1:24; 8:2; 9:7; Gal 5:22; Phil 1:25; Col 1:11; 1 Thess 1:6.

9. Rom 12:12, 15; 2 Cor 6:10; Phil 1:18; 2:17–18; 3:1; 4:4; Col 1:24; 1 Thess 5:16.

10. 2 Cor 4:15; 9:11–12; Eph 5:4; Phil 4:6; Col 2:7; 4:2; 1 Thess 3:9; 1 Tim 2:1; 4:3–4.

11. Rom 1:8; 14:6; 1 Cor 1:4; 14:17; 2 Cor 1:11; Eph 1:16; 5:20; Phil 1:3; Col 1:3, 12; 3:17; 1 Thess 1:2; 2:13; 5:18; 2 Thess 1:3; 2:13; Phlm 4.

12. In Greek, the three words are related etymologically: *chara* (joy), *eucharistia* (thanksgiving), *charis* (grace).

13. Eph 1:6, 12, 14; Phil 1:11; 4:8; cf. Rom 15:11.

14. Rom 11:36; 15:6–9; 16:27; 1 Cor 6:20; 10:31; 2 Cor 1:20; 4:15; 8:19; Gal 1:5; Eph 3:21; Phil 1:11; 2:11; 4:20; 1 Tim 1:17; 2 Tim 4:18.

15. Eph 4:1; Phil 1:27; Col 1:10; 1 Thess 2:12;

16. Rom 12:1.

THE LORDSHIP OF CHRIST

The recognition that Jesus is Lord imposes an additional obligation. As we have already noted,[17] confessing Christ as Lord must be more than a mere formal acknowledgment of who he is; it must be a personal confession of a person's submission to him. Believers acknowledge that their lives no longer belong to themselves but to Christ. By dying for them, Christ has claimed them for himself. So they can no longer live simply for themselves and their own desires; now they live for Christ,[18] and everything they do is done in his name:

> We don't live for ourselves, and we don't die for ourselves. If we live, it is for the Lord that we live; and if we die, it is for the Lord that we die. So whether we live or die, we acknowledge that we are claimed by the Lord. This is why Christ died and rose to life—so he could be Lord over the living and the dead. (Rom 14:7–9)

> He died for all of us, so that we would live no longer for ourselves but for him who died and was raised to life for us. (2 Cor 5:15)

> Everything you do or say, then, should be done in the name of the Lord Jesus, as you give thanks through him to God the Father. (Col 3:17)

This self-renouncing commitment to live for the Lord is simply following the example of Christ himself, who gave up everything to obey God's will for his life:

> Your attitude should be like Christ's . . . He freely gave up everything he had and became like a slave . . . He humbly and obediently submitted to God's will for his life, even to the point of dying—dying on the cross. (Phil 2:5–8)

Everything a Christian does, then, is to be done for the Lord. Even slaves are to perform their mundane duties out of devotion to Christ as Lord:

> Slaves, obey your human masters in everything . . . with your whole heart, out of reverence for the Lord. Whatever you do, do it with all your heart, as something you do for the Lord, not

17. See p. 20.

18. Rom 6:1–14; cf. 6:15–23, which speaks of the commitment to obedience and righteousness that results from this.

just for people . . . For Christ is the real master you serve. (Col
3:22–24)

For Paul, even the most distasteful of tasks can become an expression of
worship, if it is done out of love for the Lord.

In a few cases, specific ethical commands are to be obeyed simply
because they are decrees of the Lord.[19] Although these commands are not
many, the sharp contrast Paul draws between them and his own advice[20]
suggests that the commands of the Lord are to be regarded as the final
authority, sufficient in themselves to motivate ethical behavior without
further appeal.

Submitting to the lordship of Christ, however, is not like submitting
to a bully. The Lord is no tyrannical dictator cracking a whip over the
heads of his fearful subjects. He is a loving master, and his grace and mercy
move believers to respond in grateful allegiance to him.

THE LOVE COMMANDMENT [21]

All of a believer's relations to others (especially fellow members of the
Body of Christ) are to be motivated by love.[22] Love is not simply a feeling
or an emotion but the active expression of heartfelt, sacrificial care.

Love is of supreme importance for Paul. The greatest of the Christian virtues, love is the single most important ethical characteristic of a
Christian's life. More important than any of the popularly desired spiritual
gifts,[23] love is the moral quality with which believers are to clothe themselves above all else.[24] Listed first in "the fruit of the Spirit," love is the
mark par excellence of the Spirit's work in a person's life.[25] Viewed as both
summing up and fulfilling the moral law of the old covenant, as we have
already observed,[26] the expression of love is the one unending obligation
that believers owe to others: "Owe no one anything—except the unending
obligation of showing love" (Rom 13:8). Because the command to love

19. 1 Cor 7:10; 9:14; 14:37.

20. 1 Cor 7:10, 12, 25.

21. This section reflects ideas found in Mohrlang, "Love."

22. 1 Cor 16:14.

23. 1 Cor 12:31—14:1.

24. Col 3:14.

25. Gal 5:22–23; cf. Rom 5:5.

26. See pp. 66, 75.

others was such a large part of Jesus's own teaching, Paul speaks of it as "the law of Christ."[27]

Perhaps the best single-phrase summary of Paul's understanding of the Christian life is "faith that expresses itself in a life of love."[28] Faith and love together sum up the essence of a believer's response to Christ. Faith in Christ is the key to salvation, and loving others is the principal way that faith is lived out.[29] (Love lies at the very heart of Paul's understanding of ethical righteousness.) Paul's special emphasis on these two can be seen at the beginning of several of his letters, where he expresses gratitude for his readers' faith and love especially.[30] Love is so expressive of a person's relation to Christ that, in Paul's understanding, those who are full of love will be judged blameless and perfect on the day of Christ's return.[31]

Love is possible because those who embrace Christ step into a radically new way of life, driven no longer by selfish, sinful desires but by the Spirit of God. Love is not a self-generated social virtue but "the fruit of the Spirit"[32]—the expression of a life filled with the Holy Spirit, who pours God's own love into the believer's heart.[33] The absence of love therefore brings into question the presence of God's Spirit in a person's life—and hence the person's relationship to Christ.[34]

Loving others is simply following the example of Christ, who, out of love, gave up everything to die for us. When Paul speaks of Christ's love, his focus is not on his earthly life and ministry, but on his sacrificial death as the supreme expression of love—and the ultimate expression of God's own love.[35] And when he speaks of following the example of Christ, it is the self-sacrificing love expressed in his suffering and death to which he typically points.[36] Thus, husbands are to show their wives the same kind of sacrificial love shown on the cross by Christ, who "loved the church

27. 1 Cor 9:21; Gal 6:2; cf. John 13:14; 15:12, 17; 1 John 3:23.

28. Gal 5:6.

29. Cf. John 13:34–35.

30. Eph 1:15; Col 1:4; 1 Thess 1:3; cf. 3:6; 2 Thess 1:3; 1 Tim 1:5; Phlm 4–5.

31. Phil 1:9–11; 1 Thess 3:12–13.

32. Gal 5:22.

33. Rom 5:5; cf. Gal 4:6–7.

34. Cf. Rom 8:1–14.

35. Rom 5:8; 8:31–39; Eph 5:2; cf. 2 Thess 2:16.

36. Rom 15:1–5; 1 Cor 11:1; Eph 5:2, 25; Phil 2:5–8; 3:10; cf. 2 Cor 4:10; 8:9; Col 3:13.

and gave himself up for it."[37] Authentic Christian love, then, is always self-sacrificing, long-suffering love[38]—Christlike love. Sacrificial love of others is the believer's response to the sacrificial love shown by Christ himself.[39]

Because Christian love is always sacrificial in nature, believers must be willing to give up their own personal freedoms or rights for the sake of others:

> If you hurt a fellow believer because of something you eat, you are no longer acting in love . . . So we must always aim for those things that bring peace and that help strengthen one another . . . It is wrong to eat anything that will cause someone else to fall into sin. The right thing to do is to keep from eating meat, drinking alcohol, or doing anything else that will make another believer fall. (Rom 14:15–21)

> So then, if what I eat is likely to make a believer sin, I will never eat meat again. I don't want to make any believer fall into sin. (1 Cor 8:13)

> Try to avoid causing problems to anyone—Jews, gentiles, or the church of God. Do as I do: I try to please everyone in everything I do, not thinking of what I want but of what is best for them, so that they may be saved. (1 Cor 10:32–33)

Christians are to live not for themselves but for the good of others, and all their relations with others are to be marked by love.

When people embrace Christ, they are born into a fellowship of love, the church.[40] When Paul talks about loving others, his primary (though not exclusive) focus is on loving those in the church, one's brothers and sisters in Christ.[41] In the fellowship of Christ's people, love is of supreme importance. Love is what binds the Body together in perfect harmony,[42] enabling Christians to live together in unity and peace.[43] As members of

---

37. Eph 5:25.

38. Rom 14:21; 15:1–3; 1 Cor 6:7; 8:13; 9:12, 19–22; 10:28, 33; 13:4–7; Eph 5:25.

39. Rom 15:1–7; 1 Cor 11:1; 2 Cor 8:8–9; Eph 5:25; Phil 2:5–8; Col 3:12–14.

40. Rom 12:10; Eph 4:2, 32; Col 3:12–14; 1 Thess 4:9–10.

41. Rom 12:10, 13; Gal 5:13; Eph 1:15; 4:2, 15–16; Phil 2:1–2; Col 1:4; 1 Thess 4:9–10; 2 Thess 1:3; Phlm 5.

42. Col 3:14.

43. Rom 12:14–16; 14:19; 15:5–6; 1 Cor 1:10; 2 Cor 13:11; Eph 4:3–6, 13; 6:23; Phil 1:27; 2:2; Col 2:2; 1 Thess 5:13; 1 Tim 2:2; cf. Paul's frequent invocation, "Grace and peace be yours . . ."

one another, believers are to show grace to one another,[44] care for one another,[45] and devote themselves to building one another up in love.[46] They are to care for the poor among them, sharing sympathetically and generously with those in need.[47] Believers are to devote themselves to doing all the good they can,[48] especially to those in Christ's family—that is their first priority.[49]

But if the love commandment is taken as the guiding principle of life, it will inevitably be expressed in care for *all* who are in need, whether they are believers or not. Caring for others (whoever they are) is a reflection of God's own love; *agape*, by its very nature, has no limits. So even though Paul's primary emphasis is on the expression of love in the Body of Christ, believers driven by the love commandment will have a heart to express that love to everyone.

Finally, it is worth noting that Paul's classic chapter on love (1 Corinthians 13) occurs in the middle of a passage about spiritual gifts, written to a church that was infatuated with the gift of tongues especially.[50] His point is that the expression of love surpasses the value of any spiritual gift; moreover, without love, spiritual gifts are meaningless and ineffective.[51] In contrast to the spiritual gifts, love has unending value—love is eternal. Of all the qualities that are to characterize Christians, love is the one that most deeply reflects the nature of God himself.[52]

THE THINGS THAT HAVE ETERNAL VALUE

As people who have stepped into the Kingdom of God, Christians have entered the dimension of the eternal. Living in the anticipation of Christ's return, they should no longer live for the things of this soon-passing world but for the things of heaven, the things that last forever:

---

44. Rom 14:1—15:6.

45. Rom 12:15–16; 1 Cor 12:25–26.

46. Rom 14:19; 15:2; 1 Cor 8:1; 14:3–5, 12, 26; Eph 4:12, 16, 29; Phil 2:4; 1 Thess 5:11; cf. 2 Cor 10:8; 12:19; 13:10.

47. Acts 20:35; Rom 12:13–16; 1 Cor 16:1–2; 2 Cor 8–9; Gal 2:10; 1 Tim 6:18; Titus 3:14.

48. Titus 2:14; 3:1, 8, 14.

49. Gal 6:10; 1 Thess 5:15; cf. John 21:15–17.

50. 1 Cor 12:1—14:40.

51. 1 Cor 12:31—13:3.

52. 1 Cor 13:8–10.

> There is not much time left, so from now on married people should live as though they were not married . . . and those who deal in the things of the world, as though they were not fully occupied with them. For this world, as it is now, will not be around much longer. (1 Cor 7:29–31)

> We fix our attention not on the things that are seen but on the things that are unseen. The things that can be seen last only for a time, but the things that cannot be seen last forever. (2 Cor 4:18)[53]

> [The enemies of Christ's cross] think only about the things of the world. We, however, are citizens of heaven, and we eagerly wait for the coming of our Savior, the Lord Jesus Christ, from there. (Phil. 3:19–20)

> You have been raised to life with Christ, so set your hearts on the things of heaven, where Christ is . . . Fix your minds on the things of heaven, not on things here on earth. For you have died and your life is now hidden with Christ in God. Your real life is Christ, and when he appears, you will appear with him and share his glory. (Col 3:1–4)

For Christians, this world is no longer home, and they should not be taken up with all its attractions. Their eyes are to be focused on what lies beyond this life. The seriousness with which Paul takes this can be seen in his strong advocacy of the single life in 1 Corinthians 7. In part because the world will not be around much longer,[54] Christians (at least those who are able to live a celibate life[55]) should consider giving up even marriage for the sake of serving Christ single-mindedly.[56] The things of Christ, the things of eternity, surpass the importance of anything in this world. This emphasis gives a sense of otherworldliness to Paul's view of the Christian life.[57]

Here the idea of eternal rewards as a motivating factor enters into Paul's thinking—but only peripherally. Seeking to encourage believers to endure and to be faithful in their ministries, Paul appeals to certain unspecified rewards that faithful believers will receive beyond this life, and

---

53. Cf. 2 Cor 5:6–8.

54. 1 Cor 7:29–31.

55. 1 Cor 7:1, 7–9.

56. 1 Cor 7:32–35.

57. Cf. John Bunyan: "The Milk and Honey is beyond this Wilderness" (*Grace Abounding to the Chief of Sinners*, 4).

warns of the possibility of losing them.[58] He even speaks of salvation itself as a prize to be won.[59]

Given his apocalyptic worldview and the nature of the gospel as a message of eternal life,[60] it is not surprising that Paul expresses little interest in the wider problems of society per se. Although he instructs Christians to care for the needs of others and to do all the good they can, nowhere does he explicitly encourage them to tackle problems of injustice in the culture. Overall, Paul doesn't take it as his calling to publicly challenge the cultural norms of the Greco-Roman world. Although he criticizes the religious and moral perversions of the pagan world in his writings[61] and encourages believers to live in a way that is distinctly different, reflecting Christlike attitudes and behavior in all they do,[62] he doesn't attempt to right the wrongs of society. His concern is rather with the proclamation of the gospel and the life of the church—the work of bringing people to Christ and building believers up in him. His concern is with a different society—the society of Christ's people—and with the things of eternal importance.

Nonetheless, in their immediate neighborhoods, believers are encouraged to do all the good they can, seeking to meet the needs of the people around them.[63] "In Christ Jesus, God has created us for a life of doing good" (Eph 2:10), Paul writes. As people driven by the love commandment, Christians are to devote themselves to doing good as part of their witness to the world—an expression of the divine *agape* that has redeemed their lives.[64] Inevitably, their distinctively different lifestyle and care for others will have an effect on the world around them. Whether it is the kindness Christian masters show their slaves,[65] the care believers express for their widows,[66] the love Christian husbands show their wives

---

58. 1 Cor 3:8, 12–15; 4:5.

59. 1 Cor 9:24–25; Phil 3:10–14.

60. Titus 1:1–2.

61. Rom 1:18–32; 1 Cor 1:18—3:20; 5:9–11; 6:9–10; 10:20; Gal 5:19–21; Eph 2:1–3; 4:17–19; Phil 3:18–19; Col 2:8–23; 1 Thess 4:3–5; 2 Thess 2:3–12; 1 Tim 1:9–10; 2 Tim 3:1–9.

62. See Eph 5:21—6:9; Col 3:18–25; cf. Phlm 10–20.

63. Gal 6:9–10; 1 Thess 5:15; 2 Thess 3:13; 1 Tim 2:10; 5:10; 6:18; Titus 2:7, 14; 3:1, 8, 14; cf. Eph 2:10; 2 Thess 2:17; 2 Tim 2:21; 3:17.

64. See pp. 111–14.

65. Eph 6:9; Col. 4:1; Phlm 16–21.

66. 1 Tim 5:3–16.

and children,[67] or the compassionate way believers relate to one another generally,[68] the world around them will take notice and be affected.

THE WILL OF GOD

Sometimes Paul seeks to motivate Christian behavior by a straightforward appeal to the will of God—the obligation to live in obedience to God, in accordance with Scripture. Because the moral aspects of the Law continue to reflect the will of God,[69] the need for obedience to the moral law is presupposed in all his moral and ethical instruction.[70] The fact that God has purchased believers for himself by the death of Christ only increases their obligation; they no longer belong to themselves but to him.[71] Moreover, because his Spirit now lives in them, they must take special care to avoid anything that would offend his holy presence.[72] In everything, they must be obedient to the will of God, who has claimed them for himself and now lives within them.

THE THREAT OF JUDGMENT

Finally, when necessary, Paul has no hesitations about invoking the threat of God's judgment. For those who choose to remain outside God's grace in Christ, the eschatological judgment of God is certain. Paul speaks frankly of the coming judgment of God on those who refuse to believe the truth and freely indulge in sin,[73] those who have no love for the Lord,[74] those who have no concern to obey the gospel of Christ,[75] and all those who oppose the gospel.[76]

And when the occasion demands it, he can be equally strong in warning *Christians* of the danger of God's judgment. Note the threat of

---

67. Eph 5:25–33; 6:4; Col 3:19, 21.

68. 1 Cor 13; Eph 4:15–16; 4:31—5:2; Col 3:12–14.

69. Rom 2:21–22; 7:7; 13:9; Eph 6:2–3; cf. Rom 7:8–13; 1 Cor 7:19; see p. 75.

70. For example, Eph 4:17—5:17; Col 3:5–17; 1 Thess 4:1–8.

71. Rom 6:18–22.

72. 1 Cor 6:19–20; 2 Cor 6:14—7:1; Eph 5:7–11.

73. 2 Thess 2:12.

74. 1 Cor 16:22.

75. 2 Thess 1:8–9.

76. Phil 3:18–19; 1 Thess 2:16; cf. Gal 1:8–9; 5:10; Phil 1:28.

judgment inherent in his warnings against falling into idolatry, sexual immorality, and complaining;[77] against hurting Christ's church;[78] and against living a life of sin and wrongdoing generally.[79] The threat of judgment is also present (though less explicitly) in his exhortations of Christians to live in the fear of God[80] and in his desire that they be found blameless on the day of Christ's return.[81] Believers too will be held accountable by God.[82]

As we have noted, some of his strongest words are directed against professing believers whose lives are dominated by their sinful desires. Such people, he asserts, will have no part in the Kingdom of God; their lifestyle renders their confession of faith meaningless.[83] Professing believers who turn away from the gospel will also be condemned as unbelievers. Hence, Paul strongly warns the Galatian churches that those who put their trust in the Law of Moses cut themselves off from Christ and thereby exclude themselves from God's grace.[84] And those who undermine the faith of others by teaching this perversion of the gospel deserve special condemnation.[85]

It is clear that Paul prefers to motivate Christian behavior by more positive considerations, based on a person's relation to Christ and the gospel. But he is enough of a pragmatist to resort to the most fundamental of motivations when the occasion demands it. If professing believers don't take seriously the gospel or God's demands for holy living, Paul has no qualms about warning them in the most straightforward way of the coming judgment of God. God's grace in Christ is not to be taken lightly.

THE POINT . . .

The wide-ranging considerations to which Paul appeals to motivate Christian behavior—the saving grace of God in Christ, the authority of Christ as Lord, the love commandment, the eternal nature of spiritual verities, the moral will of God—show how deeply his understanding of Christian

77. 1 Cor 10:1–12, 22.

78. 1 Cor 3:16–17.

79. Gal 6:7–8; Col 3:25.

80. 2 Cor 7:1; Phil 2:12; Col 3:22; cf. 4:1.

81. Rom 13:11–14; Phil 1:10; 1 Thess 3:13; 5:23.

82. Rom 14:10, 12; 1 Cor 3:13–15; 2 Cor 5:10.

83. 1 Cor 6:9–10; Gal 5:19–21; Eph 5:5; cf. Rom 8:6, 13; Col 3:5–6; see pp. 102–3.

84. Gal 5:2, 4.

85. Gal 1:8–9.

living is rooted in the believer's relationship to Christ and the gospel. As those who owe Christ everything, Christians must no longer live simply for themselves and their own happiness but for Christ and his interests, recognizing that he has claimed them for himself. Their whole life is to be a joyful expression of gratitude for God's grace—a way of saying "Thank you" for all he has done for them in Christ.

Although Paul has no compunction about using the threat of judgment when the occasion demands it, his preference, clearly, is for Christian living to be motivated not by legalistic obligation and fear but by joyful gratitude to God, a sense of indebtedness to Christ, and love for others. For Paul, love is the quintessential mark of Christian faith and life. Summing up God's deepest moral desires, sacrificial love for others is simply the appropriate response of believers to the love God has shown them on the cross.

Paul's words challenge us to think much more deeply about what we live for, and why we do the things we do. Too often, our motivation reflects little more than the mores and thinking of the churches in which we grow up (some legalistic, some indulgent) and the self-centered values, priorities, and norms of our materialistic culture. As those claimed by the Lord Jesus Christ, however, we are called to live for distinctly different things than the world around us lives for. Every part of our life is to be devoted to Christ, the work of Christ, and the people of Christ; nothing is more important. As Paul puts it, "The whole point of living is Christ—Christ is everything!" (Phil 1:21).

15

The New Family of Christ

THOSE WHO EXPERIENCE GOD's redeeming work in their lives are never intended to live in isolation, apart from the Christian community. When they embrace Christ, they are born into a new family, the fellowship of Christ's Body, the church. From that moment on, the church is to play a key role in their Christian life.

In the New Testament, the term *church* (in Greek, *ekklēsia*[1]) doesn't refer to a building or a denomination but to a community of believers. In Paul's writings, the term refers both to the worldwide community of Christians[2] and to the local gathering of believers, usually meeting in someone's home. Large cities like Rome might have had several groups of Christians meeting in different homes (some, in all probability, still grouped according to traditional ethnic and social distinctions).

THE OLD TESTAMENT: A LARGELY JEWISH COMMUNITY

In the Old Testament, the people of God were those who acknowledged Yahweh as Lord and submitted to his rule and commandments. Ethnically, they were largely Jewish, though some gentile converts had joined them,

---

1. In Greek, *ekklēsia* was the word generally used for a formal gathering of people.

2. 1 Cor 10:32; 12:28; 15:9; Gal 1:13; Eph 1:22; 3:10, 21; 5:23–32; Col 1:18, 24; 1 Tim 3:15.

especially in the synagogues of the Greco-Roman cities. They considered themselves to be God's chosen people, the blessed recipients of divine mercy—those uniquely selected by God to be his people in the world. As such, they were to live in a way that was distinctly different from that of the pagan world around them and to keep themselves from being corrupted (religiously and morally) by their pagan neighbors.

Although part of Yahweh's purpose for the people of Abraham was that they be a blessing to the world—"a light to the nations," declaring his name and will to the gentiles[3] with the expectation that one day they too would come under his rule—missionary work seems not to have been greatly emphasized in Judaism. There is little evidence that Jews were ever widely engaged in outreach to the gentile world. Thus, in the Old Testament, the people of God included few people who were not Jewish.

THE NEW TESTAMENT: A WORLDWIDE FELLOWSHIP

Everything changed with the coming of Christ, who envisioned a worldwide mission expressing God's concern for the salvation of all people.[4] Accordingly, following the conversion of a key Roman army officer along with his relatives and close friends,[5] the early Christians began to proclaim the Good News of salvation in Christ to gentiles as well as Jews. The first large-scale evangelization of gentiles took place in the metropolis of Antioch in Syria.[6]

Following his conversion and call to preach the Good News, Paul came to realize that the people of God now comprise *all* who trust in Jesus as Savior and commit their lives to him, regardless of their ethnicity.[7] In Christ, the Prophet Isaiah's vision of salvation extending to all people has come to fulfillment.[8] Christ came not only to fulfill the promises God made to the Jewish ancestors but also to bring salvation to the gentiles, just as the Scriptures foretold.[9] In Ephesians especially, Paul spells out

3. See Gen 12:1–3; 18:18; Ps 67; cf. Deut 4:6; 1 Kgs 8:60; Isa 9:3–4; 42:6.

4. Matt 28:18–20; Mark 16:15–16; Luke 24:46–48; Acts 1:8.

5. Acts 10:1–48.

6. Acts 11:19–21.

7. Eph 3:1–11; cf. Col 1:26–27.

8. Isa 42:6; 49:6. In the Old Testament, God's concern for gentiles is most fully expressed in Isaiah (2:2–4; 25:6–8; 42:1–7; 45:22–24; 49:6–8; 51:4–5; 56:6–8; 60:1–3; 66:18–20, 23); cf. Gen 12:1–3; Ps 67; Mic 4:1–4.

9. Rom 15:9–12, alluding to Deut 32:43; 2 Sam 22:50; Ps 18:49; 117:1; Isa 11:10.

how the cross of Christ has destroyed the traditional enmity between Jews and gentiles and abolished the regulations in the Law of Moses that kept the two strictly separate. In Christ, God has done something new, revealing his long-hidden plan to unite Jews and gentiles as the new "Israel of God"[10]—part of his larger plan to unite the entire creation under the lordship of Christ.[11]

The home fellowships that sprang up as a result of Paul's missionary work, then, included both Jews and gentiles. When tensions erupt between the two, Paul emphasizes their equal standing before God and the importance of Christians learning to live together in unity and love, whatever their ethnic or social background.[12] He speaks of the church as a new eschatological family, a multiethnic community of believers ruled by love.[13] The traditional social and ethnic distinctions are no longer significant: "There is no difference between Jews and gentiles, or slaves and free people, or men and women. In God's eyes, you are all the same in Christ Jesus" (Gal 3:28).[14] When believers come together, they celebrate not their diversity but their unity in Christ.[15]

IMAGES OF THE CHURCH

Paul uses several metaphors to describe this new community:

The church as a family. When people come to faith in Christ, they become part of a new family, the family of God[16]— the community of all those who have been adopted by God as his children and designated as his heirs.[17] In this new family, they come to recognize fellow believers as their true

10. Gal 6:16; cf. Eph 2:14–22; 3:6.

11. Eph 1:9–10.

12. Rom 14:1—15:13; Gal 3:26–29; Eph 2:11—3:6; Phil 2:1–4; Col 3:11.

13. Rom 12:9–10; 13:8–10; 1 Cor 13:1–13; 16:14; Gal 5:6, 13–14; Eph 4:15–16; 5:2; Phil 2:1–2; Col 2:2; 3:14; 1 Thess 3:12; 4:9–10; 1 Tim 1:5.

14. Cf. Col 3:11; Phlm 1.16.

15. In Paul's letters, ethnic and cultural diversity is to be *accepted* more than paraded, and social distinctions are to be transcended. The only expression of diversity that is celebrated is the diversity of spiritual gifting (1 Cor 12). There is no encouragement of theological or moral diversity, in view of God's revelation of himself in Scripture and the gospel.

16. Gal 6:10; Eph 2:19; 1 Tim 3:15.

17. Rom 8:16–17; Gal 3:29; 4:6–7; Eph 1:5; Titus 3:7.

brothers and sisters,[18] those with whom they will live together eternally. As brothers and sisters, believers are to relate to one another in love, with genuine concern, care, and humble respect for one another, in a spirit of unity.[19] Their membership in this new family is a major part of their identity.

The church as a body. Paul compares individual believers to the various parts of a body, the Body of Christ, each with its own special work to do: "Together you are the Body of Christ; each one of you is a part of it" (1 Cor 12:27).[20] Just as a human body is dependent on the working of each part, so the church is dependent on the ministry of each member. No one is unimportant, and believers are to recognize and appreciate the contribution of every person in the Body. All believers are given specific gifts and abilities and are to use their particular contributions to build up the Body of Christ; that is the purpose of their gifting.[21] As the head of this Body, Christ is the one who makes the Body grow and works through it to accomplish his work in the world.[22] As each part of the Body matures, the fellowship of believers becomes more like the head, Christ himself:

> So we shall all become . . . mature people, fully like Christ himself. (Eph 4:13)

> In every way, we must grow to be more and more like Christ himself, the head of the Body. (Eph 4:15)

The New Testament churches were not organized around ordained pastors or priests, as many churches are today. Paul's letters speak of two levels of leadership: elders (leaders) and deacons (helpers), the latter possibly including women.[23] Although recognized leaders are sometimes mentioned, no distinction is drawn between ordained clergy and lay people. Instead, as we have noted,[24] ministry is understood much more broadly as the calling of everyone. Every believer is endowed by the Spirit with some special gifting for serving Christ in the church or the world. (The specific gifts mentioned by Paul in his four lists vary; none of the passages provides

---

18. Cf. Jesus's words in Mark 3:31–35.
19. Eph 4:2–5, 13, 32; Phil 2:1–4; Col 3:12–14.
20. Cf. 12:12–31.
21. 1 Cor 12:4–11.
22. Col 2:19.
23. 1 Tim 3:1–13; cf. 5:9–11; Titus 1:5–9.
24. See p. 92.

a comprehensive list.[25]) The church is portrayed as a mutually interactive Body with many different parts working together.

According to Paul's instructions in 1 Corinthians, when believers come together, they are to bring what the Spirit has given them individually (a psalm, a teaching, a specific word from God, or a message in tongues or its interpretation) and share it with the others.[26] In this way, everyone is involved in building up the Body.[27] Christians don't meet together primarily to worship (as we think of it today) or to hear a sermon. They come together to hear what the Spirit of God is speaking to them through one another, for their edification. They also come together to remember Jesus's death by sharing in the Lord's Supper.[28]

We assume this charismatic form of ministry was practiced in other churches established by Paul as well. But Paul doesn't discuss the issue at length in other letters. (Other letters include only a few references to the gift of speaking a specific word from God.[29]) He addresses the issue of spiritual gifts in 1 Corinthians because the church in Corinth seems to have become excessively fascinated with one particular gift, the gift of tongues. This is why Paul reminds the Corinthian believers of the full range of God's gifts and the comparatively greater value of other gifts, especially the gift of speaking a specific word from God.[30]

Cultural norms of the times seem to have restricted women's roles in ministry. Although women may pray publicly and speak a word from God to the believers,[31] Paul discourages their participation in public teaching and church leadership.[32] In general, women are encouraged to dress modestly, be quiet, live a pious and holy life, tend to the needs of the people around them, and focus on taking care of their families.[33] In everything, they are to show respect to their husbands (and husbands are to love their wives).[34] Some women (either with their husbands or individually), however, appear to have played key roles in spreading the gospel and hosting

25. See Rom 12:6–8; 1 Cor 12:7–10, 28; Eph 4:11–12.

26. 1 Cor 14:26–33.

27. 1 Cor 12:7; 14:4–5, 12, 26.

28. 1 Cor 11:17–34.

29. 1 Thess 5:20; 1 Tim 1:18; 4:14; cf. 2 Tim 1:6.

30. 1 Cor 14:1–25.

31. 1 Cor 11:5,13.

32. 1 Tim 2:12.

33. 1 Cor 14:34–35; 1 Tim 2:9–15; 5:14; Titus 2:4–5.

34. 1 Cor 11:5–12; Eph 5:22–24, 33; Col 3:18–19; 1 Tim 2:11–14; Titus 2:5.

fellowships in their homes.[35] Some young women and widows may have chosen to remain free of marriage in order to serve Christ more fully, in line with Paul's advice;[36] but what their role in ministry would have been as single women is not clear. Older widows seem to have been active in service-oriented ministries in the church.[37]

In many parts of the world today, cultural norms are less restrictive regarding women's ministry. As might be expected, given the diversity of the worldwide church, contemporary Christians differ in the extent to which they interpret Paul's words about women's roles in light of the culture of his time or as universal for all times.

The church as a sanctuary. When believers put their trust in Christ personally, the Spirit of God comes to reside in them individually; their bodies become sanctuaries.[38] In the same way, when believers meet together, they function as a sanctuary collectively.[39] The Spirit "baptizes" believers into this fellowship,[40] and the Spirit is the bond that unifies them in it.[41] The church of God, then, is not just a collection of ordinary people; it is nothing less than a holy fellowship uniquely inhabited by God himself:

> All of you surely know that you are the sanctuary of God and that God's Spirit lives in you! . . . Together you are God's holy sanctuary. (1 Cor 3:16–17)

> We are the sanctuary of the living God! As God himself has said, "I will make my home in them and live among them. I will be their God, and they shall be my people." (2 Cor 6:16)

> Christ is the one who holds the building together and makes it grow into a holy sanctuary for the Lord. In him you too are being built into a place where God lives by his Spirit. (Eph 2:21–22)

As the sanctuary of God, the church is to be a genuinely holy community, demonstrating the transformed way of living that characterizes regenerated people. Sin has no place in the church; believers are to address

---

35. Acts 16:14–15, 40; 18:26; Rom 16:1–15; 1 Cor 16:19; Col. 4:15; Phlm 1–2; cf. 2 Tim 4:21.

36. 1 Cor 7:8, 17–40.

37. 1 Tim 3:11; 5:9–10 may refer to women who serve as deaconesses.

38. 1 Cor 6:19.

39. 1 Cor 3:16–17; 2 Cor 6:16; Eph 2:21–22.

40. 1 Cor 12:13.

41. Eph 4:3.

sin seriously but in love.[42] Living together in the unity of the Spirit, they are to avoid doing anything that would hurt or divide the church.[43] The way Christians relate to one another in holiness, humility, unity, and sacrificial love is part of their witness to the world.

Without question, even with all of its failings, Paul has a high view of the church. Filled with the Spirit of Christ, the community of believers is the fullest expression of Christ that can be seen in this world—"Christ's Body, the full expression of the One who completely fills the universe with his presence" (Eph 1:23). The presence and glory of Christ in it should be perceivable to everyone. The church is to be a trophy displaying the magnificence of God's redeeming work to the entire universe.[44] The life of the church and the way its members relate to one another are to be a tangible witness to the message it proclaims to the world.

The church as the bride of Christ. In Ephesians, discussing the relation of husband and wife, Paul draws a comparison with Christ and the church. A wife is to submit respectfully to her husband as her "head," just as the church submits to Christ as its head. The husband, for his part, is to love his wife sacrificially, just as Christ loved the church and gave up his life for it. Christ sacrificed himself to purify the church and dedicate it wholly to himself. His desire was to make the church his pure and beautiful bride, immaculate and flawless. Moreover, because the church is now his bride, with its individual members united to him as part of his Body, he provides and cares for its every need.[45] Here Paul portrays the worldwide church as inexpressibly precious to Christ—the love of his life.

These four metaphors (the church as a family, a body, a sanctuary, and the bride of Christ) reveal Paul's high view of the church. They help us to understand why he is so deeply concerned that believers live in unity and love,[46] reflecting God's grace and glory in all they do. The church is God's witness to the world, and its members are Christ's representatives. Every part of their life together is to reflect the transforming influence of Christ and to show the world the reality of the living God who dwells among his people.

42. 1 Cor 5:1–13; Gal 6:1; 1 Tim 5:20.

43. See 1 Cor 3:17.

44. Eph 2:7; 3:10.

45. Eph 5:21–33.

46. Rom 15:5–6; 1 Cor 1:10–13; 12:12–26; 13:1–13; Gal 5:13–15; Eph 4:1–6; Phil 2:1–11; Col 3:13–15.

"SACRAMENTS"

Paul's letters speak of two rituals associated with the life of the church: baptism and the Lord's Supper. Both of these, as expressions of sharing personally in the death of Jesus, are powerful reminders of the central significance of the cross in the Christian faith. Differing interpretations of these rituals have divided the Christian community. Churches differ in the understanding of the nature, function, and importance of baptism and the Lord's Supper, and of the way they are to be practiced. (The Roman Catholic Church, with its highly developed sacramental theology, speaks of seven sacraments, not two.) Those with a high view of the rituals as holy sacraments think of them as special means of receiving God's grace. Others prefer to speak of them as ordinances and think of them more simply as expressions or signs of grace rather than as special means of receiving grace.

What do these rituals signify to Paul, and how important are they in his thinking?

Baptism. In the earliest Christian community, it was generally adults, not children, who were baptized,[47] and baptism was typically by immersion in water. Baptism served both as a public expression of a person's commitment to Christ and as a kind of initiation rite into the fellowship of believers. People were usually baptized at the time of their conversion, often on the same day.

Paul doesn't seem to place a great deal of theological importance on the physical act of baptism itself:

> I thank God that I did not baptize any of you except Crispus and Gaius . . . (Oh yes, I also baptized Stephanas and his family; I cannot remember whether I baptized anybody else.) Christ did not send me to baptize but to proclaim the Good News. (1 Cor 1:14–17)

On the other hand, Romans 6 (the passage where he talks most about baptism) could leave the impression that Paul is a strict sacramentalist (one who believes that the ritual is essential for salvation):

---

47. Only three passages leave open the possibility of children being baptized by Paul: Acts 16:15, 33; 1 Cor 1:16—each of which speaks of a family or household being baptized, without specifying who is included. Infant baptism seems not to have been widely practiced in the church until a later time.

> Don't you know that when we were baptized into Christ Jesus, we were baptized into his death? When we were baptized, we died and were buried with him, so that, just as Christ was raised from death by the glorious power of the Father, we also might live a new life. Since we have become united with him by dying as he did, we shall also be raised to life as he was. (Rom 6:3–5)

But in my judgment it is unlikely that Paul thinks of the physical act of baptism itself as the effective means of joining a person to Christ. More significant to him seem to be the personal identification with Christ's death and Resurrection that baptism expresses and the inner experience of being "baptized by the Spirit."[48] As a rule, he emphasizes that it is by trusting in Christ and confessing him as Lord that a person is saved—*this* is what is essential. But because baptism typically occurred at the time of a person's conversion, we can understand how baptismal language came to be linked with the experience of conversion, especially since baptism itself symbolizes conversion. (Going down into the water symbolizes going into one's grave, that is, dying to sin with Christ; coming up out of the water symbolizes being resurrected from the dead, that is, arising to live a new life with Christ.[49]) So although Paul says it is "through baptism" that a person is united with Christ in death and resurrection, the phrase is best interpreted as meaning "through the personal faith and commitment that baptism expresses." Baptism and conversion always go together in Paul's thinking; but the conversion seems to be what is important to Paul, more than the outward act of baptism itself.

If we may draw a parallel with circumcision under the old covenant, Paul's view of circumcision also seems to reflect a non-sacramental way of thinking:

> Just because you live like a Jew outwardly and are circumcised physically doesn't make you a real Jew. A real Jew is one who is a Jew on the inside, and real circumcision is something that happens deep in your heart—by the work of God's Spirit, not the written Law. (Rom 2:28–29)

> It doesn't matter at all whether you are circumcised on uncircumcised. The only thing that matters is keeping the commandments of God. (1 Cor 7:19)

48. 1 Cor 12:13.
49. See Rom 6:3–5.

For Paul, the important thing is not the physical circumcision itself but the inner commitment it expresses.[50] In the same way, the important thing seems to be not the outward rite of water baptism per se (of which he speaks relatively little) but the trust in Christ and the commitment that it signifies. If the physical act of baptism itself were the actual means of salvation, we would expect him to have emphasized it much more and to have expressed its saving nature more explicitly.

But this is not to say that baptism is unimportant or optional. In the New Testament, baptism is the standard way that believers publicly confess their faith in Christ and their commitment to him, and a sign of their entry into the community of the new covenant.

The Lord's Supper. Similarly, there is little to suggest that Paul has a strongly sacramental view of the Lord's Supper (Holy Communion, the Eucharist). Only two passages in all of his letters refer to the Supper.[51] In these passages, the Lord's Supper serves as the following:

- an expression of personally sharing in the body and blood of Christ[52]

- an expression of union with other believers in the Body[53]

- a means of remembering Christ's sacrifice on the cross[54]

- a way of proclaiming the redeeming message of Christ's death[55]

The Lord's Supper is a personal and corporate reliving of the death of Jesus in the life of the church—the expression of the new covenant of God by which the church lives and dies.

On the surface, the wording could be interpreted as strictly sacramental:

> The cup of blessing . . . , is it not our sharing in the blood of Christ? And the bread we break, is it not our sharing in the body of Christ? (1 Cor 10:16)

> He took some bread . . . and said, "This is my body . . . This cup is the new covenant in my blood . . . " So if you eat the bread or drink the wine in a way that is not worthy of the Lord, you are

50. Cf. Rom 4:11, where Paul speaks of Abraham's circumcision as a "seal" (confirmation) of the righteousness by faith that he had even before he was circumcised.

51. 1 Cor 10:16–17, 21; 11:1–16.

52. 1 Cor 10:16.

53. 1 Cor 10:17.

54. 1 Cor 11:23–25.

55. 1 Cor 11:26.

> guilty of sinning against the body and blood of the Lord . . . For
> if you don't recognize the Lord's body when you eat the bread
> and drink the wine, you invoke God's judgment on yourself
> when you eat and drink. (1 Cor 11:23–29)

But both passages allow for a broader, non-literal translation, as some versions prefer:

> The cup of blessing . . . , is it not *an expression of* our sharing in
> the blood of Christ? And the bread we break, is it not *an expression of* our sharing in the body of Christ? (1 Cor 10:16, emphasis
> added)

> He took some bread . . . and said, "This *represents* my body . . .
> This cup *represents* the new covenant in my blood . . . " So if you
> eat the bread or drink the wine in a way that is not worthy of
> the Lord, you are guilty of sinning against the body and blood
> of the Lord . . . For if you don't recognize *the significance of* the
> Lord's body when you eat the bread and drink the wine, you
> invoke God's judgment on yourself when you eat and drink.
> (1 Cor 11:23–29, emphasis added)

For Paul, personal faith in Christ and commitment to him—not the mere
outward expression of it—is the means by which a person comes to receive
salvation. As with baptism, if Paul thought of the Lord's Supper itself as
mediating salvation, we would expect him to have emphasized it much
more and to have expressed its saving nature more explicitly.

But this is not to say that the Lord's Supper is to be taken lightly. In
light of the sacred event it symbolizes, Paul cautions, those who fail to take
it seriously invoke God's judgment on themselves—physical weakness,
sickness, and even death. (But he doesn't imply that a person is thereby
excluded from salvation.) The reliving of the Lord's atoning death for the
sins of the world, and God's new covenant through it, must never be taken
lightly. Many have found the experience of taking the Lord's Supper to be
a helpful means of personalizing the significance of Jesus's death, and not
a few have found the assurance of salvation through it.[56]

In any case, Paul's warning about God's judgment on the Israelites
in the desert makes it clear that neither baptism nor the Lord's Supper
in itself guarantees salvation. Even though the Israelites were "baptized"
into Moses and had their own form of Holy Communion (sharing in the

---

56. "In moments of doubt, to see, to touch, to share, and to eat and to drink constitute an assurance, a pledge, a promise, and an 'effective sign' of covenant grace" (Thistleton, *The Living Paul*, 125).

provision of Christ), most of them fell dead under the judgment of God because of their sin.[57] Paul clearly intends the reference as a warning for his baptized readers.

As Paul's letters portray it, then, the life of the church is not so much sacramental as *charismatic*; it is to be guided and empowered by the Spirit in all it does.

THE POINT . . .

In our individualistic society, growing numbers of those who call themselves Christians are turning away from the church, regarding it as irrelevant to their lives. Some are highly critical of the church and even find it an embarrassment (sometimes, with good reason). Its glaring problems and failings, frequently paraded in the media, are more obvious than its glory.

Moreover, of those who do identify with the church, many have little understanding of themselves as vital, ministering parts of the Body of Christ. For many, ministry is largely the work of those who are ordained, and "church" means little more than the passive observance of Sunday morning services. For some, church attendance is little more than family tradition or the obligatory receiving of the sacraments.

Paul's ecclesiastical metaphors reflect a much higher view of God's church. For Paul, the worldwide church is the chosen family of God. It is the sanctuary of God's Spirit, the special fellowship inhabited by God himself in this world. The church is the living Body of Christ, with every believer playing an active and vital role in its ministry. And it is the much-loved bride of Christ, for whom the Savior died. Indeed, the worldwide church is *the fullest expression of Christ that can be seen in this world*. As such, every part of its life and ministry is to reflect the glory of Christ himself, who lives in it and works through it—for all to see. In every way, the life of the church is to be energized and guided by the Spirit of God and characterized by the expression of love. Paul's high view of the church strongly challenges our more mundane and worldly ways of thinking about it, and any passive understanding of our role in it.

57. 1 Cor 10:1–6.

16

What Lies Beyond Death?

How does Paul the Christian think about the experience of death and what lies beyond it? How did his experience of the resurrected Christ change his traditional Jewish perspective on the end of life?

JEWISH PERSPECTIVES

According to the Old Testament, Jews traditionally believed in the nebulous, gloomy place called Sheol[1]—the world of the dead, where the spirits of the dead (both righteous and unrighteous) were understood to reside. But by New Testament times, many Jews were distinguishing between paradise, where the righteous dead were considered to reside, and Sheol, which was reserved for the unrighteous, as they awaited the Day of Judgment.[2] Paul probably grew up recognizing this distinction.

As a Pharisee, however, he also grew up believing in the future Day of Resurrection,[3] when God would raise from the dead those who were righteous and receive them, with new spiritual bodies, into his presence.[4]

---

1 Hebrew *šě'ôl*; Greek *hadēs*.

2. Cf. Luke 16:19–31.

3. Unlike Pharisees, Sadducees did not believe in a future resurrection.

4. Although Dan 12:2 suggests that both the righteous and the unrighteous will rise at the end of time (one to eternal life, the other to eternal shame), early Jewish literature varied in its understanding of whether the unrighteous would be included in the future resurrection.

No one, however, could count with absolute certainty on being among those blessed ones; in Judaism, the best one could do was hope.

CHRISTIAN PERSPECTIVES

As a result of his experience of the resurrected Christ, Paul's view of the afterlife (especially for believers) became sharper and more certain. His letters reflect a joyful, confident anticipation of the future Day of Resurrection for those who belong to Christ.[5] Committed believers can count with confidence on living in the world beyond with new resurrection bodies like that of their Savior[6]—and Jesus's own Resurrection is the reality that confirms that.[7] The future resurrection of Christ's people will then mark the ultimate victory over the last great enemy, death.[8]

But what happens to believers who die before the coming resurrection? Where will they be in the interim? Paul doesn't say a great deal about the experience of believers immediately beyond death, even in the passage where he addresses the question most explicitly—perhaps because he is so convinced that Christ will be returning soon:

> I want you to be aware of what will happen to Christians who have died, so you will not grieve over them like people without any hope. Just as we believe that Jesus died and was raised to life, so we believe that God will raise those who have died believing in him, along with him . . . The Lord will return from heaven, and those who have died believing in Christ will be raised to life first. Then we who are still living at that time will be raised in the clouds with them, to meet the Lord in the sky. From that time on, we will be with the Lord forever. (1 Thess 4:13–17)

Because Paul speaks of the dead as those who have "fallen asleep,"[9] some argue that Paul believes in a state of soul sleep for dead believers prior to their awaking in the future resurrection. But here falling asleep is more likely a euphemism for dying that is not intended to be taken literally.[10]

---

5. 1 Thess 4:13–18.
6. 1 Cor 15:35–49.
7. 1 Cor 15:20–23.
8. 1 Cor 15:26, 51–57.
9. 1 Cor 7:39; 11:30; 15:6, 18, 20, 51; 1 Thess 4:13–15.
10. Cf. John 11:11–14, where Jesus explains his own use of this euphemism.

An important passage in Philippians suggests that Paul does *not* think of the dying Christian's spirit as entering a state of soul sleep. In this passage, Paul weighs the comparative advantages of continuing to live in this world and dying:

> The whole point of living is Christ—Christ is everything! And dying will bring something even better . . . I don't know which to choose; I am torn in two. I would really like to die and go to be with Christ—that is the better option. But for your sake, it would be better if I stayed around for a while. (Phil 1:21–24)

The passage makes sense only if Paul believes that death will carry him immediately into the presence of Christ. (This belief would seem to fit the idea of eternal life better than the notion of soul sleep does.) This is good news for any believer who is dying. The passage is puzzling, however, because it makes no mention of a future resurrection.

IMMEDIATE TRANSFER OR FUTURE RESURRECTION?

So how do these two ideas—the notions of a future resurrection and an immediate transfer to the presence of Christ—fit together? Some scholars conclude that Paul's view must have changed after he wrote the passage about resurrection in 1 Thessalonians 4, but there is little evidence to support this. It is more likely that he came to assume a two-stage view of life beyond death (as many later Christians did), in which the believer's spirit (1) goes to be with Christ at the point of death and (2) is later united with a new resurrection body when Christ returns.

But a puzzling passage in 2 Corinthians leaves some scholars wondering whether his thinking about the *timing* of the future resurrection changed (that is, moved forward to the time of a believer's death) as he became more aware that he himself might die before the return of Christ:

> We know that when the time comes for our earthly tent to be torn down, we will have a new building waiting for us in heaven—not a human home but an eternal home, made by God. As long as we are here on earth, we sigh with longing for our heavenly home. We want to be clothed with that home, so that we may not be found naked. As long as we are in our earthly tent, we groan—it weighs us down. We don't just want to get rid of our mortal body; we want our mortality to be swallowed up by life! This is what God has prepared us for, and the Spirit he has given us is the guarantee.

So be encouraged—always! As long as we are at home in this earthly body, we are away from our home with the Lord . . . We would rather leave the home of our earthly body and be in our home with the Lord. Whether we are in our home here or there, however, our aim is to please him. For Christ will judge each one of us for the good or bad we do while living in these bodies. (2 Cor 5:1–10)

In this enigmatic passage, the heavenly "building" or "home" that believers will receive in place of their earthly "tent" (body) seems to be expected the moment they die. But the precise meaning of the heavenly building is not clear: is this the resurrection body, an interim resurrection body, a heavenly residence, the full experience of salvation, full eschatological glory, or something else?[11] Nor is the degree of precision intended in the chronology clear. In any case, what Paul emphasizes is the glory that awaits believers beyond this life, in contrast to the imperfections of their present earthly existence. The uncertainty of the details and the imprecise chronology should keep us from assuming too quickly that Paul changed his mind about when believers receive their resurrection body.

THE JOYFUL HOPE AND ULTIMATE ACCOUNTABILITY

The anticipation of Christ's return and the final resurrection is the great Christian *hope* that Paul proclaims so strongly[12]—the confident, joyful assurance believers have of one day sharing in the full experience of God's glory. Christians, then, are neither to fear death nor to be anxious about fellow believers who have died.[13] Those who trust in the Lord can rest assured that death will open for them the door to a life with Christ that far transcends anything they will experience in this world—"something even better."[14] And as citizens of heaven, they can look forward to the coming of their Savior from heaven and the full transformation they will experience

---

11. Margaret Thrall lists nine different interpretations of the "heavenly building": *The Second Epistle to the Corinthians*, 363–67.

12. Rom 5:2–5; 8:23–25; 12:12; 15:13; 1 Cor 13:13; Eph 1:18; 4:4; Col 1:5, 23, 27; 5:8; 1 Thess 1:3; 5:8; 2 Thess 2:16; Titus 1:2; 2:13; 3:7; cf. 1 Cor 1:7; Gal 5:5; 1 Thess 1:10; 2 Tim 4:8.

13. 1 Thess 4:13–18.

14. Phil 1:21.

when he comes.[15] The joyful anticipation of the Second Coming is a key part of Paul's grand view of the future.

The triumphal tone of all this, however, is tempered somewhat by the awareness that the coming Day of the Lord brings with it the Day of Judgment, when every human being (believers included) will be held accountable by God.[16] Because nobody knows exactly when that day will come, Christians must live seriously, in constant readiness for it, not carelessly presuming on their salvation.[17] So faithful believers live in a state of paradoxical tension: while confidently anticipating the coming of Christ and the glory of the life beyond, they also live out their salvation in the fear of God,[18] conscious of the seriousness of one day standing before the final judge. Even though they have the reassuring presence of God's Spirit and don't live in mortal fear, as if they were unbelievers,[19] they must still live reverently before God,[20] knowing that the promises of God are only for those who remain true to the End. A. W. Tozer expresses the balance nicely: "The greatness of God rouses fear within us, but His goodness encourages us not to be afraid of Him. To fear and not be afraid—that is the paradox of faith."[21]

THE "RAPTURE"?

What about the various eschatological categories (pretribulational, midtribulational, posttribulational, premillenial, amillenial, postmillenial) that are used by Christians to define different interpretations of the End Times and the timing of the "rapture" (the coming of Christ to take his people to be with himself) or the Second Coming?[22] Which of these describe Paul's view of the End?

Nowhere does Paul give us a detailed, comprehensive analysis of the End Times that would enable us to define the chronology of his eschatology precisely. All we have are isolated bits of eschatological references in

15. Phil 3:20–21.

16. See pp. 36, 104–5.

17. Rom 13:11–14; 1 Thess 5:1–11.

18. Phil 2:12.

19. Rom 8:15.

20. Rom 11:20–22; 2 Cor 5:11; 7:1.

21. *The Knowledge of the Holy*, 84.

22. For a popular description of these terms, see the *Wikipedia* article "Christian eschatology."

various passages, dealing with different issues.[23] Without going into detail, what can we conclude from these passages?

- Because he doesn't refer to the millennium, it is impossible to define Paul's view of the End as premillennial, amillennial, or postmillennial—or even millennial at all.[24]

- He seems to believe that an apocalyptically difficult time for the world is coming before Christ's future return.[25]

- He seems to speak of only one future coming of Christ, associated with the Day of Resurrection—not two;[26] he makes no clear distinction between a "rapture" and the Second Coming.

- His emphasis is not on knowing the precise time of Christ's sudden return but on the importance of being constantly ready for it—by living a holy life, so that one will be prepared (morally and spiritually) for the accountability it brings.

- Those who are faithfully committed to Christ can anticipate the Day of Resurrection with joy and confidence.

Paul might actually find some of the eschatological categories and End Times scenarios of contemporary Christians quite strange. His focus and concerns are different from those of much popular eschatology today.

THE POINT . . .

When believers die, their spirits live on in the presence of Christ. Then on the future Day of Resurrection—whose timing cannot be easily predicted but for which believers must be constantly prepared because it brings with it the Day of accountability—they will receive new spiritual bodies and will live forever with Christ, sharing the full glory of God. So death holds no fear for those who stake their lives on the Good News and remain faithfully committed to Christ. For them, the experience of death will bring unspeakable joy and, one day, a much fuller experience of the glory of God than they have ever known.

23. The main passages are 1 Cor 15:20–58; 2 Cor 5:1–10; 1 Thess 4:13—5:11; 2 Thess 2:1–12.

24. The only New Testament reference to the millennium is in Rev 20:2–7.

25. 2 Thess 2:1–12.

26. See 1 Cor 15:12–58; 1 Thess 4:13–18.

Paul's eschatological focus calls into question our earthbound perspectives. Today, we easily find ourselves taken up with the transitory things of this comfortable world in which we live. For most of us, the present world is a much larger part of our thinking and priorities than the world beyond; eternal issues frequently don't enter into our considerations.

But Paul is much more focused on the great Christian hope and the exciting prospect of what lies beyond this life. For him, this glorious hope is a source of irrepressible joy in the midst of all the world's difficulties. His words encourage us to remember the temporal nature of the present world and to keep our eyes fixed on the ultimate goal. The finally important things are those that last forever, not the mutable and transient things of this life.

17

Paul's Evangelism and Ministry

IT WOULD BE INADMISSIBLE to end this study of Paul without considering his remarkable life as a missionary-apostle for Christ. Here we take a
closer look at his evangelistic and pastoral work and the seriousness of his
dedication to the work of Christ.

HIS COMMITMENT TO CHRIST

Paul's letters leave the striking impression that his life is wholly dedicated
to serving the resurrected Lord and his mission. Nothing else matters very
much. Because the message he proclaims is a message of eternal life and
his ministry focuses on the ultimate issues of life, the ephemeral things of
this world hold little interest for him:[1]

> All those things I once thought so important, I now consider
> worthless for Christ's sake. Indeed, I consider everything worth-
> less in light of what is so much more valuable, the experience
> of knowing Christ Jesus my Lord. For his sake, I have given up
> everything else—it is all garbage—so that I may get Christ and
> be found in him . . . All I want now is to know Christ and to
> experience the full power of his Resurrection in my own life, to
> share in his sufferings, and to die as he did. (Phil 3:7–10)

1. 2 Cor 4:18; cf. his admonition of Timothy not to let himself become preoccupied
with the practical matters of ordinary life: 2 Tim 2:4.

The one thing of supreme importance is Christ and his work in the world. Because Paul owes his life to Christ and knows that Christ has claimed him for himself, his desire is to devote his entire life to serving the Lord Jesus:

> My deep desire and hope is that I will never be ashamed but that I will always—even right now!—boldly bring honor to Christ with my whole life, whether I live or die. To me, the whole point of living is Christ—Christ is everything! (Phil 1:20–21)

> My own life means nothing to me. My only desire is to faithfully complete my mission and the work the Lord Jesus has given me to do—the work of proclaiming the Good News of the grace of God. (Acts 20:24)

Because of his dedication to Christ, his life and priorities have a laser-sharp focus rarely seen in others.[2] He is single-minded in his commitment to the work of Christ, regardless of the suffering it entails. Even the sacrosanct traditional goals of marriage and family are sacrificed for Christ.[3]

HIS MISSIONARY EVANGELISM

Right from his conversion, Paul felt personally called by God to be his missionary.[4] His strong sense of calling can be seen in the way he introduces himself as "a missionary-apostle chosen and called by God to preach his Good News."[5] Nine of his thirteen letters begin with an emphasis on his divine calling, highlighting his God-given authority. In line with Jesus's word to him at his conversion,[6] he took as a specific word from God for himself a Scripture that the early Christians typically applied to Jesus: "I have made you a light to the nations, so that the whole world may be saved" (Acts 13:47).[7] This powerful sense of calling gives boldness to his proclamation and strength to his exhortation and rebuke.[8] As Paul tells

---

2. Phil 3:12–14.

3. 1 Cor 9:5; cf. his recommendation of the single life in 1 Corinthians 7.

4. Acts 9:15–16; 22:15, 21; 26:16–18.

5. Rom 1:1.

6. Acts 26:18.

7. Cf. Luke 2:32.

8. Rom 15:15–16; 1 Cor 4:21; 5:3–5; 2 Cor 10:2–6, 12; 11:5, 12–15; 12:11, 13:2, 10; Gal 1:8–9; 2:14; 5:12; 2 Thess 3:12; 1 Tim 1:20; cf. 1 Tim 1:3–4; 5:20; Titus 1:13; note

Timothy, those commissioned by the Lord to do his work must be strong and bold—indeed, fearless—if they are to serve him faithfully.[9]

Behind Paul's dedication to missionary evangelism lies a deep-seated conviction that the world is lost.[10] This conviction gives a sense of urgency to his mission work. Drawn especially to proclaim the Good News to people who have never heard it,[11] he longs to see those who are lost brought to God.[12] This missionary emphasis, with its focus on the desperate need of the world for salvation, is radically different from anything he knew in Judaism.

Paul speaks of his calling to evangelize gentiles as part of God's *mystery* that has now finally been revealed—his long-secret plan to incorporate gentiles into his family.[13] Paul sees himself as chosen to play a key role in that divine plan.[14] Believing that he is living in the Last Days and that Jesus will be coming back soon,[15] he understands his proclamation of the gospel to gentiles to be a strategic part of the events associated with the End.

The seriousness with which Paul takes his missionary work can be seen in two passages especially, both of which reflect his sense of responsibility for the fulfillment of his calling. The first comes from Luke's account of Paul's parting words to the leaders of the church in Ephesus, the second from his words to the Corinthians:

> So I tell you today, if any of you end up lost, I am not responsible. I have held nothing back; I have told you everything God wants you to know. Remember that, day and night, for three whole years, I taught every one of you, with tears in my eyes. (Acts 20:26–31)

> I have been commanded to preach the Good News—and I am doomed if I don't! (1 Cor 9:16)

the strong tone of Galatians and 2 Corinthians 10–13 especially.

9. 2 Tim 1:7–8; 2:1,3; 4:1–2, 5.

10. See p. 36.

11. Rom 15:20–21.

12. Cf. 2 Cor 5:20: "On behalf of Christ, we plead with you to be reconciled to God!"

13. Rom 16:25–26; Eph 1:9–10; 3:3–6, 9–11; cf. 2:12–22. He speaks more generally of God's secret plan in Rom 11:25; 1 Cor 2:1, 7; 4:1; Eph 6:19; Col 1:26–27; 2:2; 4:3.

14. Eph 3:1–8; cf. Col 1:25–28.

15. 1 Cor 10:11; 1 Thess 4:17.

His dedication can also be seen in the extent to which he is prepared to adapt his lifestyle to that of his hearers, in the hopes of winning them for Christ:

> I make myself everybody's slave, so that I can win as many people as possible. When I am among the Jews, I live like a Jew to win Jews . . . When I am among gentiles, I live like a gentile . . . to win gentiles . . . So I adjust my lifestyle to that of the people I am trying to reach. I do everything I can to win every person I possibly can. (1 Cor 9:19–22)

> I try to please everyone in everything I do, not thinking of what I want but of what is best for them, so that they may be saved. (1 Cor 10:32–33)[16]

Note that it is his *lifestyle* that Paul adapts, not the message of the gospel or the ethical teachings of Scripture. For Paul, neither theology nor ethics are appropriate matters for adaptation—those are matters of divine revelation.[17] It is matters of *form, not substance, that require adaptation.*

Doing whatever is required so that people may be saved is more important to Paul than simply pleasing himself. He is committed to living sacrificially for the sake of the gospel, so that, whatever it takes, people may come to know God's forgiving grace. And he devotes himself tirelessly to this task.

What about believers generally? Does Paul expect every Christian to be an evangelist like himself? The short answer is no. Not all believers are called to be evangelists, in the strict sense of the word,[18] but all *are* called to be active witnesses—that is, to have a missionary heart and lifestyle. Paul is delighted when believers share the Word of God openly and fearlessly with others.[19] Like stars brilliantly lighting up the night sky, Christians are to shine the light of Christ to those living in darkness around them.[20] As Christ's representatives in the world, they are to live in a way that brings honor to the gospel, and to do nothing that would detract from their

---

16. Cf. his concern with the church's witness in 1 Thess 4:11–12; 1 Tim 5:14; 6:1; Titus 2:2–10.

17. Note Paul's refusal to compromise the central message of the gospel in 1 Cor 1:22–23; cf. his strong defense of the gospel in Galatians, and his clear ethical warnings in 1 Cor 6:9–10; Gal 5:19–21; Eph 5:5–6; Col 3:5–6.

18. Eph 4:11.

19. Phil 1:14; 2:16.

20. Phil 2:15; cf. Eph 6:15.

witness.[21] Practically, this means they are to have the reputation of being quiet, modestly dressed people who work hard.[22] Their family life is to be exemplary, and they are to take good care of their relatives in need.[23] They are not to be known as criticizers or belligerent people but as gentle, gracious, kind people,[24] responding amicably and respectfully even to those who oppose them.[25] They are to have a reputation for doing good and meeting people's needs.[26] Their witness is to be expressed in their lives as well as their words.

HIS MINISTRY TO CHRISTIANS

Paul's work as a missionary-apostle involves discipleship as much as evangelism.[27] Just as he devotes himself to bringing people to Christ, so he devotes himself to instructing and encouraging young believers. Here too, the intensity of his dedication is unmistakable. Like a woman suffering labor-pains, he agonizes to see the full life of Christ formed in his converts.[28] He is as concerned for their welfare as mothers and fathers are concerned for their children, and he invests himself deeply in caring for them.[29] He labors individually over young converts so that each one may become mature in Christ.[30] He is willing to endure no end of suffering for their sake.[31]

Paul speaks of himself as a servant of the church for Jesus's sake[32]—indeed, as one of the very few who are more concerned for Christ's church than for their own interests: "All the others are concerned only for their

---

21. 1 Cor 10:32–33; 1 Thess 4:11–12; 1 Tim 5:14; 6:1; Titus 2:2–10; note especially verses 5, 8, 10.

22. 1 Thess 4:11–12; 2 Thess 3:6–12; 1 Tim 2:9–10.

23. 1 Tim 5:3–16.

24. Titus 3:2.

25. Rom 12:14, 17–21; cf. 13:7.

26. Gal 6:9–10; 1 Thess 5:15; 2 Thess 3:13; 1 Tim 2:10; 5:10; 6:18; Titus 2:7, 14; 3:1, 8, 14; cf. Eph 2:10; 2 Thess 2:17; 2 Tim 2:21; 3:17.

27. Cf. Matt 28:18–20.

28. Gal 4:19.

29. 1 Thess 2:7–8, 11–12; 3:10.

30. Col 1:28.

31. Phil 2:17; 2 Tim 1:12; 2:9–10.

32. 2 Cor 4:5.

own interests, not those of Jesus Christ" (Phil 2:20–21)—an unusually critical assessment for Paul.

His deepest desires for Christian converts are expressed in his prayers in the Prison Letters,[33] where he prays that they will come to the following:

- a deeper understanding of God, his desires, his promised blessings, and his Resurrection power at work in their lives

- an awareness of the full greatness of Christ and his love

- a greater experience of love, spiritual discernment, purity, the character of Christ, and the power of God's Spirit

- a life that is increasingly pleasing to God in every way

His primary concern is not simply for their physical welfare (to which he refers very little) but for their *spiritual* life—the deepening of their experience of God, Christ, and the Holy Spirit, and the full expression of this in all their relationships. He longs for them to be filled with the life and power of God himself.[34]

Paul is intentional about wanting his own life to be an example for others. On a number of occasions, he instructs his readers to imitate his ways: "Follow my example, just as I follow the example of Christ" (1 Cor 11:1).[35] Much of what he writes about himself is intended to serve as a model for them. Indeed, he writes, all Christian leaders are to live exemplary, unimpeachable lives that can serve as models for other believers.[36] And one of the keys to this way of life, he implies, is the serious reading of Scripture.[37]

More than once Paul feels it necessary to defend his character. Aware of some of the rumors being spread about him, he reminds his readers that he has been a person of absolute integrity in all his dealings with them.[38] This is one of the major themes of 2 Corinthians especially, where Paul defends himself against the criticism of those who oppose him.[39] His concern is not just for his own reputation; the gospel and the work of Christ

33. Eph 1:15–23; 3:14–19; Phil 1:9–11; Col 1:9–14.

34. Eph 3:19.

35. Cf. 1 Cor 4:16; Phil 3:17; 2 Thess 3:7, 9; 2 Tim 1:13; 3:10–11, 14.

36. 1 Tim 3:1–13; Titus 1:5–9; cf. 1 Tim 4:12.

37. Cf. 1 Tim 4:13, where Paul encourages Timothy to devote his time especially to the (public?) reading of Scripture, and to the exhortation and teaching of God's people; cf. 2 Tim 3:15–17.

38. 1 Thess 2:3–12; 2 Tim 3:10–11.

39. 2 Cor 1:12—2:4, 17; 3:17; 4:2, 5; 5:11–15; 6:3–10; 7:2, 12; 8:20–21; and especially 10:1—13:10.

are at stake. He knows that a life of transparent integrity is essential for the sake both of his evangelism and of his ministry to Christians.

HIS DEDICATION TO GOD'S WAYS

Paul has learned that God's truth and God's ways of doing things are different from the world's ways.[40] In all his evangelism and ministry, he wants his critics to know that he doesn't follow the world's ways of thinking and doing things, and that the world's traditions mean little to him.[41] He emphasizes that his missionary calling and message don't derive from human beings but from Christ himself.[42] The gospel he preaches is not an ordinary human message,[43] and the seeming ridiculousness of it stands in sharp contrast to the supposed wisdom of the world. But the gospel has a divine power to convert people that the world's wisdom doesn't have;[44] God's way of teaching truth differs from the more intellectual ways of the world.[45] So Paul doesn't fight his spiritual battles using ordinary human weapons:

> Even though we live in the world, we don't fight the way the world does. We don't use the world's weapons but God's powerful weapons, and with them we destroy the opposition, no matter how strong they may be. (2 Cor 10:3–4)

Nor does he rely on mere human strategy or motivation when he engages in ministry.[46] In every respect, Paul wants his readers to know that God's truth and God's ways transcend ordinary human ways of thinking and doing things,[47] just as God's power transcends ordinary human power.

Paul has "died" to the world and its ways, and the world is now "dead" to him.[48] Just as he himself no longer evaluates people by ordinary human

---

40. Greek *ta stoicheia tou kosmou*, "the world's ways" (Gal 4:3, 9; Col 2:8, 20; cf. 2:18–23).

41. Rom 2:28–29; Eph 2:11; Col 2:8.

42. Gal 1:1, 11–12.

43. 1 Thess 2:13; 4:8.

44. 1 Cor 1:18–25; 3:18–19.

45. I Cor 2:1–16.

46. 1 Cor 15:32; 2 Cor 1:12, 17–18; 10:2–3.

47. 2 Cor 7:10.

48. Gal 6:14.

standards,[49] so he is no longer concerned with what others think of him from a mere human perspective: "I don't care what you or anyone else thinks of me" (1 Cor 4:3). He has no desire simply to please others.[50] The people whom God chooses to make his own are not those the world would choose,[51] and Paul wants all his relations with them to be governed not by human norms but by God's norms.[52] In Christ, he has come to a different way of thinking and valuing, and he seeks to express that in all he does.

HIS RESPONSE TO SATAN

Well aware of the unseen spiritual realm and the reality of demonic powers (see Luke's account of his exorcism in Acts[53]), Paul realizes that his opposition derives ultimately from the world of spiritual evil: "We are not fighting against human beings but against the forces of evil in the spiritual world—the rulers, authorities, and cosmic powers of this dark age" (Eph 6:12). He is keenly sensitive to the spiritual world and the opposition of the Evil One to the work of God. His is no naturalistic view of the world.

In Paul's world, human beings are not so much autonomous agents making rational decisions on their own, as people driven by spiritual forces more powerful than they are. His reference to the Devil as "the god of this world" reflects his belief in the wide-ranging nature of Satan's power and influence. As "the god of this world," the Devil blinds the minds of unbelievers[54] and dominates their lives.[55] Able to disguise himself as a servant of God,[56] Satan has the potential to undermine the results of Paul's evangelism[57] and to interfere with his pastoral work.[58] Immature, worldly Christians are especially susceptible to his traps.[59] Christians, then, must be wise in all their dealings in order to keep Satan from getting the better

---

49. 2 Cor 5:16.
50. 1 Cor 4:3; Gal 1:10.
51. 1 Cor 1:26–31.
52. 2 Cor 1:12.
53. Acts 16:16–18.
54. 2 Cor 4:4
55. Eph 2:2.
56. 2 Cor 11:14.
57. 1 Thess 3:5.
58. 1 Thess 2:18.
59. 1 Tim 3:6–7.

of them.[60] Drawing on all that God has given them in the gospel, they must protect themselves well against the Enemy's harassment.[61] Christ's people are caught up in the cosmic war between God and the ultimate source of evil.

In the strange sovereignty of God, however, even Satan is used for the greater purposes of God himself. Paul's "thorn in the flesh" is the tormenting work of Satan—but it serves God's purpose in keeping Paul humble.[62] Satan's destructive work plays a role even in God's discipline and restoration of the young Corinthian man who is having sex with his father's wife.[63] And strangely, twice Paul speaks of handing erring believers over to Satan himself (not to God) for punishment.[64] God uses even Satan for his own ends.

Ultimately, the power of Satan is subject to the limits set by God. Paul is confident that the Evil One cannot finally thwart the work of Christ.[65] In the end, Satan's doom is certain,[66] for the cross and Resurrection have sealed his fate and have demonstrated, for the entire world to see, Christ's power over him: "On that cross Christ defeated all the spiritual powers and authorities. He let the whole world see them being led away as prisoners, while he celebrated his victory" (Col 2:15).[67]

Thus, although Paul takes the reality of Satan and his opposition seriously, his life and ministry are not dominated by anxiety over Satan. Nor does his view of Christian life and ministry center on spiritual war. He speaks much more about the danger of sin than the danger of the Devil. Moreover, when he talks about spiritual war, he doesn't encourage Christians to engage in an aggressive attack against the Devil but simply to protect themselves from his insidious influence.[68] (Almost all the protective pieces of spiritual armor to which he refers are defensive in nature; only the short sword is an offensive weapon.) Paul seems to have a cautious, limited view of the Devil's influence and danger. Although the Evil One

60. 1 Cor 7:5; 2 Cor 2:11.

61. Eph 6:1–18.

62. 2 Cor 12:7–10.

63. 1 Cor 5:5.

64. 1 Cor 5:5; 1 Tim 1:20.

65. Cf. 1 John 4:4: "The One who is in you is greater than the one who is in the world."

66. Rom 16:20; 2 Thess 2:8.

67. Cf. 1 Cor 15:24–25; Eph 1:20–21; Col 2:10.

68. Eph 6:10–18.

is to be taken seriously, Christians are confidently to trust in the Lord's protection and care. For Paul, the focus of the Christian life and Christian ministry is not on the Devil and spiritual war but on Christ, the gospel of Christ, and the power of Christ's Spirit. His overall focus is positive, not negative.

THE POINT . . .

Paul's lifelong dedication to living for Christ and his work in the world stands as a remarkable example of devotion and commitment. Called by Christ personally, he takes his missionary work with the utmost seriousness and gives himself tirelessly to preaching the gospel wherever he goes. Turning from the ephemeral things of the world, he devotes himself single-mindedly to the eternal work of Jesus—evangelism, discipleship, and church planting especially. He labors unstintingly to serve the churches and bring every believer into a mature relationship to Christ. In everything he does, he wants his life to be an example for believers and a model of following God's ways, not the world's ways.

Paul's impressive example of devotion and commitment reminds us that Christ is what life is all about. It challenges us to take seriously our calling to (1) live no longer for ourselves but for Christ, his people, and his work in the world; (2) be strong, positive witnesses for Christ in all we do; and (3) take seriously the lost state of the world, and its need for Christ and the gospel. Even though we are not all called to be evangelists like Paul, all of us are called to live as Christ's witnesses and representatives in a world that doesn't know him, and to devote our lives to serving him. Nothing is more important for those who belong to him.

18

A Life of Suffering

FINALLY, ONE OF THE most impressive things about Paul's life—and a key to the fruitfulness of his ministry—is his willingness to embrace suffering for Christ. Paul's perspective on suffering stands in marked contrast to that of traditional Judaism. More troubling, it also stands in marked contrast to ours today.

OLD TESTAMENT PERSPECTIVES

In the Hebrew Scriptures, material prosperity, good health, large families, and the absence of suffering are commonly spoken of as signs of God's blessing on the righteous. Troubles and suffering, on the other hand, are often portrayed as the afflictions of the unrighteous.

Of course, there are exceptions. As Ecclesiastes reminds us, sometimes those who are evil end up vexingly rich and prosperous, while those who are pious end up poor and afflicted.[1] (Because of their special need to depend on God, the poor eventually came to be identified as God's righteous people in a distinctive sense, the recipients of his special care.[2]) Some parts of the Old Testament (for example, Job) challenge the simple-minded link traditionally drawn in Judaism between suffering and sin,[3]

1. Eccl 7:15; 8:12–14; cf. Ps 73:1–12.
2. Ps 37:14; 69:33; Isa 3:15; 29:19; 41:17.
3. See Job's responses to the accusations of his friends in 4:7; 8:4; 11:6, 13–14.

and others (for example, Jeremiah) clearly show that faithful individuals are sometimes called to a life of suffering.[4] Moreover, the Wisdom literature suggests that, to some extent, difficulties and suffering are the lot of everyone—that is simply the nature of the world in which we live.[5] Nonetheless, many ordinary Jews in Paul's time assumed that a happy, prosperous life was generally a mark of God's blessing. Suffering was not ordinarily viewed as the lot of God's faithful people.

NEW TESTAMENT PERSPECTIVES

In the early Christian writings, however, suffering is spoken of more positively, and it plays a more significant role in the life of Christ's people. It was to a life of suffering that Christ himself was called, Paul writes. He gave up his divine privileges and followed the path of obedience all the way to the cross.[6] And Christians are to imitate Christ, sacrificing their own desires for the good of others.[7] (Jesus himself said that those who wish to follow him must commit themselves to a life of self-renunciation and suffering, and be willing to die with him.[8]) The New Testament emphasis on suffering stands in sharp contrast to much of the Old Testament—and to the prosperity theology that is so popular worldwide today.

CALLED TO A LIFE OF SUFFERING

Right from his conversion, Paul was aware that his missionary calling would entail suffering.[9] The theme of suffering runs through several of his letters (especially 2 Corinthians, Philippians, and 2 Timothy). He makes it clear to his converts that suffering is part of their calling as Christians.[10] Indeed, he instructs Timothy, "Everyone who desires to live a godly life in Christ Jesus will be persecuted" (2 Tim 3:12). In the same way, according

4. See Jer 1:18–19; cf. 12:5.
5. See Job, Proverbs, Ecclesiastes.
6. Phil 2:6–8.
7. 1 Cor 11:1; Phil 2:5.
8. Mark 8:34–35; 13:9–13; John 15:18–20.
9. Acts 9:16.
10. 1 Thess 3:3–4; cf. Rom 8:17; 2 Tim 2:11–12.

to Acts, he put the believers in southern Turkey on notice that they must go through many troubles to enter the Kingdom of God.[11]

Nowhere does Paul speak of believers as being immune from suffering, and nowhere does he promise that God will protect them from it.[12] Practically, there may be times when the best thing for believers to do is simply to get out of harm's way, as Paul himself sometimes (but not always) did.[13] But when inevitable suffering comes to those who are faithful, their calling is to accept it with grace and to persevere patiently in it.[14] At such times, suffering for Christ is to be considered an honor and a privilege.[15] Indeed, it is only by sharing in the suffering of Christ that believers will come to share in his eternal glory.[16]

CONTENTMENT, PEACE, AND JOY IN SUFFERING

As a missionary in the service of Christ, Paul has come to accept adversity and to view difficulties and suffering in a positive light. So he welcomes and embraces hard times. He now sees difficulties and suffering—not prosperity—as the hallmark of faithfulness to God. He views his suffering as a mark of the authenticity of his apostolic commitment, in contrast to the pretenses of others:[17]

> Do they claim to serve Christ? I know this sounds pretentious, but I serve him better than they do! I have worked harder, and I have been put in jail more times than they have. I have been whipped more, and I have come close to dying more. Five times my own people gave me thirty-nine lashes with a whip; three times the Romans beat me with a rod; and once my enemies tried to stone me to death. I have been in three shipwrecks, and

11. Acts 14:22.

12. However, he does encourage prayer for political leaders, so that believers may live quiet and peaceful lives: 1 Tim 2:4.

13. Acts 9:23–25, 29–30; 14:5–6, 19–20; 17:5–10, 13–14; 20:1; cf. Acts 25:7–11, where Paul took advantage of his Roman citizenship to get his court case reassigned to Rome when the Jewish leaders pressured the Roman procurator to have him tried in Jerusalem. In some cases, however—out of obedience to God or a sense of God's leading perhaps—he chose not to protect himself from danger: Acts 16:20–24; 21:4, 11–13.

14. Rom 12:12; 2 Thess 1:5.

15. Phil 1:29.

16. Rom 8:17.

17. 2 Cor 6:4–5; 11:23–28; cf. Rom 8:36; 1 Cor 4:9–13; 15:30–31; 2 Cor 1:3–10; 4:7–12.

once I spent a whole day and night in the sea. In all my travels, I have been in frequent danger—from flooding, robbers, my own people, and foreigners. I have faced dangers in the cities, in the countryside, on the high seas, and from people pretending to be my friends. I have been overwhelmed with work and struggles and have had many sleepless nights. I have gone hungry and thirsty and at times have had nothing to eat. I have been cold from not having enough clothes. Besides all that, every day I am weighed down with the burden of my concerns for all the churches. (2 Cor 11:23–28)

At times, he feels overwhelmed by the burden of his work.[18] But just as his Lord accepted suffering as his calling, so Paul accepts it as his. Indeed, he speaks of longing to enter into the fellowship of Christ's suffering and to die as Christ died.[19] He wants to be like Christ in everything he does.

Paul has even come to think of his sufferings as his part in God's redemptive work in the world: "I am glad I can suffer for you. By my physical sufferings I am helping to complete what still remains of Christ's sufferings on behalf of his Body, the church" (Col 1:24).[20] He is not suggesting here that he has any part to play in the atoning work of Christ; suffering is simply part of his calling as a messenger of Christ's salvation to the world.

As a result, Paul has learned to find contentment even in the most difficult situations and to trust the Lord's provision and care:

I have learned to be satisfied with whatever I have . . . Whatever the situation—whether I have much or little, whether I am full or hungry—I have learned to be content. Christ gives me the strength to deal with anything. (Phil 4:11–13)

God's love, he is convinced, is big enough to embrace any difficulty his people encounter in this world. His love is sufficient to take everything, no matter how difficult, and turn it into good for those who love him.[21] When faithful believers experience suffering for Christ, then, they can rest assured that God will use it to strengthen them and deepen their character,[22] to make them more worthy of the Kingdom of God.[23] Ulti-

18. 2 Cor 1:8–9; 4:7–12; 11:28–29.

19. Phil 3:10.

20. Cf. Eph 3:13.

21. Rom 8:28.

22. Rom 5:3–4.

23. 2 Thess 1:5; cf. 1:11.

mately, such suffering works to make believers more like Christ himself.[24] And one day their suffering will result in incomparable glory forever,[25] just as it did for their Savior.

The upshot of all this is that faithful believers are not to be unduly concerned when they encounter difficulties beyond their control; rather, they are to rejoice. Writing from jail to Christians being persecuted in Thessalonica and Philippi, Paul emphasizes that no matter what their difficulties, they are to rejoice constantly and give thanks in everything—even their persecution. They are not to worry about anything, but to pray about everything:

> Rejoice always, pray constantly, and thank God, whatever comes your way. This is the way God wants you to live in Christ Jesus. (1 Thess 5:16–18)

> Always be joyful in the Lord . . . Don't worry about anything, but pray in every situation, asking God for what you need with thankful hearts. (Phil 4:4–6)

Even in the midst of difficulties and persecution, believers are to be Christ's joyful, grateful people.[26] No matter what assails them, they are to rejoice in God's grace and to trust in his care. (Note that Paul writes these words from *jail*.)

A deeper lesson lies hidden in this. In Paul's grace-ruled view of the Christian life, outward circumstances, no matter how difficult, should never be what determines the believer's response. Whatever the situation, a Christian's response is to be determined not by circumstances but by his or her relation to Christ. For Paul, circumstances are never to have the final say.

Paul's attitude to difficulties and suffering is reflected in his view of slavery. No matter how harsh or demanding their masters may be, Christian slaves are to do their work energetically and obediently, as an expression of their reverence for Christ, their real master.[27] Whether their human master is watching them with a critical eye is unimportant; they are to do their work not simply for their master but for Christ. (In Paul's understanding, this principle is valid not only for slaves but for all believers,

24. Rom 8:29.

25. 2 Cor 4:17; cf. Rom 8:18.

26. In 1 Thess 5:18, Paul urges believers to be grateful *in* all circumstances; in Eph 5:20, he encourages them to be grateful *for* all circumstances—an even greater expression of confidence in God's love.

27. Eph 6:5–8; Col 3:22–24; cf. 1 Tim 6:1; Titus 2:9–10.

whatever their work.) Whether a believer is a slave or a free person, then, actually doesn't matter a great deal (though Paul discourages believers from voluntarily placing themselves in slavery[28]). After all, in Christ slaves are really free, and free people are really slaves (of Christ) anyway.[29] *Real* freedom and *real* slavery are defined inwardly, not outwardly; freedom is a way of thinking and living defined by one's relation to Christ as Lord and Savior, not by one's social status. A believer's physical situation, then— even if it involves suffering—is largely irrelevant. The important thing is to live for Christ and bear witness to him, whatever the circumstances.

With all the problems the Lord's people face, Paul still encourages them to be at peace. Significantly, all thirteen of his letters begin with an invocation of God's peace, and several close with a benediction or promise of his peace.[30] Peace is God's gift to his faithful people who have learned to trust his love and his promises of care, no matter how difficult their circumstances. In the midst of all their difficulties, the God of peace[31] gives his people peace.[32]

LEARNING TO RELY ON GOD

As a result of his missionary experience and suffering, Paul came to a much deeper awareness of his need to rely on God for everything. Keenly aware of his weaknesses and human limitations (he speaks of these in 2 Corinthians especially, written shortly after his difficult two to three years in western Turkey[33]), he realizes that God has a purpose in the troubles he allows him to experience. God wants Paul to learn to trust *him* rather than himself:

> Our sufferings were so horrible and so unbearable that death seemed certain; we were sure we were going to die. But this was to teach us to trust not in ourselves but in God. (2 Cor 1:8–9)

---

28. 1 Cor 7:23.

29. 1 Cor 7:21–22.

30. Rom 15:13, 33; 2 Cor 13:11; Gal 6:16; Eph 6:23; Phil 4:9; 2 Thess 3:16.

31. Rom 15:33; 16:20; 2 Cor 13:11; Phil 4:9; 1 Thess 5:23; 2 Thess 3:16.

32. Rom 8:6; 14:17; 1 Cor 7:15; 14:33; Gal 5:22; Phil 4:7; Col 3:15; 2 Tim 2:22; cf. 1 Tim 2:2.

33. See p. 13.

Moreover, Paul came to realize that the suffering he experiences allows the life of Jesus to be seen more clearly in his body than if his life were trouble-free:

> We are like ordinary, fragile clay pots in which this treasure is stored—to show that the real power comes from God, not from us. (2 Cor 4:7)

> Every day we bear the death of Jesus in our bodies—so that the life of Jesus also may be seen in our bodies. We always face the danger of dying for Jesus's sake, so that his life may be seen in our mortal bodies. (2 Cor 4:10–11)

The message Paul preaches is embodied in his own suffering. The death of Christ is proclaimed both in his words and in his life.

Later in 2 Corinthians Paul speaks about a mysterious "thorn in the flesh" that he experienced, which he begged the Lord to take away.[34] The Lord, however, did not take it away but told him, "My grace is all you need, for my power is most effective when you are weak" (2 Cor 12:9). Here was a crucial lesson for Paul: by the power of Christ, Paul's ministry is more effective when he is weak than when he is strong. Through this painful experience, Paul came to realize that human weakness, far from being detrimental, can actually serve the cause of Christ well.[35] He concludes,

> I am glad, then, to brag about my weaknesses, so that the power of Christ may rest on me. So I am content with my weaknesses . . . and sufferings for the sake of Christ; for when I am weak, then I am strong. (2 Cor 12:9–10)

In his strange providence, God chooses to work through ordinary, weak people in difficult circumstances, so that all the glory may be his. Ironically, sometimes their weakness and limitations are exactly what God uses to make their life and ministry fruitful.

But this doesn't deny the importance of Christians seeking to be strong for Christ in all they do—as Paul repeatedly encourages Timothy to be.[36] More than once, especially when defending himself, Paul feels it necessary to emphasize his own hard work and energetic dedication to the gospel.[37] Those who serve Christ must do their work responsibly and well, for God's work and theirs are inextricably intertwined: "To this end I work

34. 2 Cor 12:7–8.

35. 2 Cor 11:30; 12:5, 9–10.

36. 2 Tim 1:7–8; 2:1, 3; 4:1–2, 5.

37. See especially Acts 20:18–31; 2 Cor 6:4–10; 11:23–28.

hard and struggle, using all the energy Christ gives me, which is at work in me" (Col 1:29).[38] The recognition that God works through weak people doesn't mean that believers should serve Christ with anything less than full strength and energy. But in doing so, they freely acknowledge that even their strength and energy come from God; *everything* is a gift of God: "For God is at work in you, giving you both the desire and the capability to do what pleases him" (Phil 2:12–13).

Through these difficulties, Paul came to realize that the effectiveness of his witness and ministry is dependent more on God's work than his own.[39] Of course, he takes his responsibility seriously and seeks to serve the Lord with all the energy and abilities God has given him; but fruitful results finally come from God himself:

> I planted the seed and Apollos watered the plant, but God is the one who made the plant grow. (1 Cor 3:6)[40]

> God's grace has made me what I am, and his grace has not been ineffectual. I have worked harder than any of the other apostles—but it has really been God's grace working with me, not just me. (1 Cor 15:10)

In Christian ministry, God and his people work strangely together;[41] but in the end, fruitfulness comes from God.[42] *God* is the one who speaks through Paul,[43] and *God* is the one who makes his evangelism and ministry effective. So Paul concludes, "Whoever wants to brag must brag about the Lord, not about himself" (1 Cor 1:31; 2 Cor 10:17).

Difficulties and suffering, then, are experiences that God uses to teach his people to rely on him, and through such trials he brings glory to himself. Christ's people are not to run away from suffering but to accept and embrace it. Believers are not called to a life of ease.

THE POINT . . .

Most of us are far removed from the suffering of the early Christians. The comfortable, affluent world in which we live and the value our culture

38. Cf. 2 Tim 2:10.
39. Col 1:29; cf. Rom 15:18–19; 2 Cor 3:5; Eph 3:7, 20; 1 Thess 2:13.
40. Cf. 1 Cor 15:10.
41. Cf. 2 Cor 5:20; 6:1.
42. Cf. 2 Tim 4:17–18.
43. 2 Cor 5:19–20; 13:3.

places on happiness and success do little to encourage a positive view of suffering. Indeed, influenced by Western media and reinforced by certain Old Testament passages, many Christians around the world think of happiness and prosperity—not suffering—as the sign of God's blessing.

In Paul's letters (and in the New Testament as a whole), however, suffering for Christ plays a much more significant role. Following the Lord's example, Christians are to embrace suffering as they commit themselves to a self-denying life of serving him—knowing that God will use such difficulties for his own purposes and for their good, to make them more like Christ. The awareness of their weakness and vulnerability only heightens their dependence on God. Encouragement comes from knowing that fruitfulness in witness and ministry is ultimately the result of his work, not simply theirs. So believers are encouraged to be joyful and grateful, and to be at peace, even in the midst of the troubles they experience for Christ. In all of life's difficulties, their response is to reflect their relation to Christ. Those who take the Lord seriously, then, are committed to living for him and his work in the world—even if it entails suffering.

How prepared are we to accept suffering for Christ?

19

A Brief Summary and Challenge

AMONG THE EARLY CHRISTIANS, Paul was truly remarkable. His contribution to the Christian faith, both as a missionary-evangelist and as a letter writer, was monumental. His life and thinking, so often different from ours, stand as a challenge to us who claim to take Christ seriously today.

Any study of the man must begin with his life-changing experience on the road to Damascus. Unexpectedly confronted by the resurrected Jesus, he found his whole life suddenly thrown into confusion, along with many of his most cherished Jewish convictions. The experience revolutionized his life. From that moment on, Paul knew that his life was claimed by Christ—the one he came to know as the Son of God and Messiah, the Lord and Savior of the world, and the final judge.

He devoted the rest of his days to serving him as a missionary. With extraordinary dedication and perseverance in the face of repeated opposition, he gave himself to proclaiming the Good News of salvation in Christ as widely as he could in the Greco-Roman world. It was a prodigious task, but Paul was convinced that it was the most important work in the world. He suffered a great deal—and eventually died—in the service of Christ and the gospel.

And what an amazing message it was—and is: the message that God, in his mercy and love—and in fulfillment of his promises in Scripture— sent his own Son to die for the world's sins, so that undeserving sinners might be forgiven and made right with him. God welcomes and accepts those who turn to him and put their trust in Christ, regardless of how they have lived. Credited with the perfect righteousness of Christ himself, faithful believers will stand free of guilt on the Day of Judgment, fully pardoned.

But another part of the message is equally astounding: the revelation that the resurrected Jesus, by his Spirit, now comes to live in those who embrace him. As a result, Christians begin to experience resurrection life themselves. Just as the Prophets predicted, the gift of salvation resolves the problem of sin comprehensively—by giving believers both *forgiveness of sin* and *power over sin*. It not only makes them right with God; it also transforms them.

Thus, Christians are no longer doomed to a life of failure and sin. Renewed by the Spirit, they can begin to live the good life that God desires, becoming more and more like Jesus himself. The key is to be filled with the Spirit of God—energized and guided by his Spirit.

Those who receive his grace must recognize that they no longer belong to themselves but to the Lord. Their whole life is to be devoted to him; nothing else is ultimately important. Everything they do is to be motivated by their experience of Christ and his grace. Full of joy and gratitude, their Christian life is to be a way of saying "Thank you" to God for the mercy he has shown them in Christ.

This new life is to be lived out not independently but in fellowship with their new family, the Body of Christ. Transcending traditional social and ethnic distinctions, Christian brothers and sisters are to care for one another and to use the special abilities God gives them to build one another up in Christ. All they do is to be done in love—this is "the law of Christ." Their life together is to be a reflection of the life of Christ in them, a light to the world. Everything they do, both individually and communally, is to bear witness to Christ and his life-giving message.

As citizens of heaven with resurrection life, Christians are not to be dominated by worldly concerns. They are to live for the things of heaven, the things of eternal value. They are to live as people of hope, with their eyes fixed on the future coming of Christ and the life beyond. And one day, like him, they will experience the indescribable joy of resurrection and eternal glory in God's presence.

Because Jesus's death and Resurrection mark the eschatological beginning of the Kingdom of God, Christians can experience here and now the life and power of the Kingdom as they await the return of Christ. But in this world they will always feel the tensions of their already / not yet kind of existence. They have to accept the eschatological paradox of living in two different dimensions (this world and the heavenly world) simultaneously. Both must be taken seriously.

They have to accept a theological paradox too—the truth that every part of their salvation is a gift of God's sovereign initiative and grace, yet still contingent on their response. They are utterly dependent on God to save and keep them, but they also know that salvation is only for those who remain faithfully committed to Christ. They live with the joyful assurance of eternal life, but also with a sense of reverential fear, knowing that one day God will hold them accountable for how they have lived. In everything, they must take seriously both the sovereign initiative of God and their own personal responsibility. They must learn to live with paradox.

Even though they live as children of grace, they are not destined for a life of ease, any more than their master was. Called to be faithful witnesses of Christ, they must accept difficulties and suffering in this world. But in all their difficulties, they have the assurance that the Lord is at work in their lives, turning their troubles into good. In all their trials, God is working in and through them for his glory and teaching them to trust *him* rather than themselves.

For believers, such a message is nothing less than stupendous. To be brought into a real experience of the living God and to be given so many amazing gifts—the assurance of his forgiving grace, the promise of eternal life, the life-transforming power of his Spirit, the joy of a truly good life, the encouragement and fellowship of Christ's people, the experience of God's love, and all his countless blessings—is all this not astonishing?

And what does God ask in return? That those who receive his gifts of grace gratefully dedicate their lives to his love and service: "So I urge you, brothers and sisters, because of the mercies of God, to dedicate your lives to him as a kind of living sacrifice, holy and pleasing to him." (Rom 12:1).

What this means, of course, is that we who claim to take Christ seriously must learn to live in a way that is distinctly different from that of the world around us. Every part of our life—our values, our priorities, our motivation, our goals, our sense of identity and purpose, our whole way of thinking and living—is to be transformed by the Spirit of God. Claimed by Christ, in fellowship with his people we are called to live confidently and joyfully as his representatives in a world that doesn't know him.

What a magnificent calling!

Paul's Letters: Brief Summaries and Outlines

NOTE: MORE DETAILED SUMMARIES and outlines may be found in study Bibles and commentaries.

Romans is, without question, the most important of Paul's letters theologically. Many Christians consider it the most important book in the New Testament, if not in the whole of Christian history.[1] Here we have the fullest and most systematic exposition of the Christian gospel in the New Testament.

The longest of Paul's letters, written (about AD 56–57) to Christian home fellowships in the capital of the empire, Romans serves to introduce Paul and his message before his planned visit to them, and (secondarily) addresses tensions between Jewish and gentile believers. The letter is divided into three major sections:

1:18—8:39. In the first section, Paul provides a full exposition of the Good News of salvation, and responds to those who might object to his view of the Law of Moses. Sin is the bane of all people, rendering them guilty before the judgment of God. Salvation, mercifully provided by the atoning sacrifice of Christ, is not a reward for proper observance of the Law of Moses but a gift of God's grace to all who put their trust in Christ to save them—gentiles as well as Jews. God's salvation provides a comprehensive answer to the problem of sin: it makes believers right with God, and it enables them to overcome sin and live a God-pleasing life by the power of the Holy Spirit.

---

1. Luther thought Romans to be so important that "every Christian should know it word for word, by heart, [and] occupy himself with it every day, as the daily bread of the soul. It can never be read or pondered too much" (Luther, *Commentary on the Epistle to the Romans*, xi).

9:1—11:36. The second section deals with the question of why the Jews have not accepted God's salvation, while many gentiles have. Paul lays out several considerations, which reveal the paradoxical nature of his thinking about God's sovereign choice and personal responsibility.[2]

12:1—16:27. In the third section, Paul describes how Christians are to live in response to God's salvation, and gives advice on two specific issues: believers' responsibility to civil authorities, and conflicting opinions over food and holy days in the church. The new life of believers is to be a response of wholehearted gratitude for the grace of God that has saved them, and is to be characterized by love for one another.

Outline:

1:1–17	Introduction
1:18—8:39	The Good News of salvation
1:18—3:20	The universal need for salvation
3:21—8:39	God's gift of salvation through Christ
9:1—11:36	What about the Jews' salvation?
12:1—15:13	Exhortation to live as Christians
15:14—16:27	Final words and personal greetings

1 Corinthians is one of at least four letters Paul wrote to the key church in southern Greece, located in the port city of Corinth. In this letter (written about AD 52–55), Paul gives advice on a wide range of problems facing this proud church, and responds to the questions they have sent. The letter shows some of the practical problems the early churches faced and the pastoral way Paul deals with them. Most important, it reveals the deepest moral and ethical principles (especially the principle of love) that shape his thinking about Christian life and community.

Outline:

1:1–9	Introduction
1:10—15:58	Advice on problems and questions
1:10—4:21	Divisiveness and criticism of Paul
5:1–13	A case of incest
6:1–11	Court cases between Christians

2. See pp. 55–56.

6:12–20	Sexual immorality
7:1–40	Marriage, divorce, and the single life
8:1—11:1	Food dedicated to pagan gods
11:2–16	Appropriate dress for women engaged in ministry
11:17–34	Problems associated with the Lord's Supper
12:1—14:40	Spiritual gifts and the priority of love
15:1–58	The future resurrection of believers
16:1–24	Final words

2 Corinthians is a lengthy defense of Paul's apostolic authority, and an emotional response to those in the church who are critical of him. In this letter (written about AD 55–56), Paul attempts to regain the believers' full confidence by reminding them of (1) his integrity and love for them, (2) how much he has suffered as a missionary for Christ, and (3) the ways God has worked through him, despite his weaknesses. In the last few chapters (10–13), he strongly challenges those who are comparing him unfavorably with other missionaries. The only major interruption occurs in chapters 8–9, where he encourages generous giving for the needs of the poor Christians in Jerusalem. The significance of the letter lies in what it reveals of Paul's understanding of ministry and its motivation, the role of suffering in it, and the way God uses outwardly unimpressive people in his service. God's ways are distinctly different from those of humans.

Outline:

1:1–11	Introduction
1:12—7:16	Explanation of Paul's motivation and ministry
8:1—9:15	Giving for poor Christians in Jerusalem
10:1—13:10	Paul's defense of his ministry and rebuke of those criticizing him
13:11–13	Final words

Galatians is a strongly worded, forceful argument against Jewish Christians who are trying to convince gentile converts in the highlands of central Turkey that they must be circumcised and observe the Law of Moses. Paul emphasizes that, according to the Good News revealed to him by Christ, salvation is a gift of God's grace for all who put their trust in Christ, not a reward for obedience to the Law. Citing both the Old Testament and Christian experience, he argues that salvation is based on faith in Christ alone and has nothing to do with the Law of Moses. Indeed, those who revert to relying on the Law forfeit all their privileges in Christ. This extended argument is followed by a brief word about the need for believers to lead a Spirit-directed life. The letter is a strong argument for justification by faith in Christ.

Outline:

1:1–10	Introduction and the problem
1:11—2:21	The divine origin of Paul's gospel and missionary authority
3:1—5:12	Salvation by faith in Christ, not by the Law of Moses
5:13—6:10	Exhortation to live a Spirit-filled life
6:11–18	Final words

Ephesians, written from prison (perhaps about AD 52–56)[3] to the key church in western Turkey (and probably to the surrounding churches as well[4]), provides a magnificent summary of the Good News of God's saving grace and one of the finest descriptions of the Christian life in the New Testament. A favorite of many, the letter is divided into two major sections. In the first section (chapters 1–3), Paul highlights the incredible grace that God has given in Christ to wholly undeserving sinners—gentiles as well as Jews—according to his long-secret plan. In the second section (chapters 4–6), very similar to the second section of Colossians, he describes the new way of life that believers are to live in response to God's grace, and then cautions them of the need to protect themselves from the Devil. Ephesians splendidly describes the wonder of God's amazing grace, now available to all, and the Christlike life that believers are to live in response.

Outline:

1:1–2	Introduction
1:3—3:21	God's amazing grace—for gentiles as well as Jews
4:1—6:20	Exhortation to live as Christians
4:1—5:20	Living in a Christlike way
5:21—6:9	Showing love and respect in Christian homes

3. See p. 8 n. 14.

4. Because several early Greek manuscripts omit the words "in Ephesus" from the address (1:1), many scholars believe this letter may originally have been a circular letter sent to churches in western Turkey, to which the reference to Ephesus was added later because of its prominence as the key city in the province.

| 6:10–20 | Protecting oneself from the Devil |
| 6:21–24 | Final words |

Philippians, written from prison (perhaps about AD 52–56)[5] to a church in northeastern Greece, is a warm letter of encouragement for believers who are suffering persecution, and an expression of thanks for the gift they have sent. Referring to his own dedication to Christ and willingness to suffer as an example for them to follow, Paul encourages them to be joyful, prayerful, and grateful as they live for Christ in the midst of persecution. Full of pastoral concern and passion for Christ, this heartfelt letter shows the strength of Paul's dedication and his willingness to suffer for Christ; it also shows that a Christian's life is to be marked by joy, gratitude, love, and determined devotion to Christ, whatever the circumstances.

Outline:

1:1–11	Introduction
1:12–26	Paul's personal circumstances in prison
1:27—4:9	Exhortation to live as Christians in an unbelieving world
4:10–20	Paul's gratitude for their gift
4:21–23	Final words

Colossians, written from prison (perhaps about AD 52–56)[6] to a church in the highlands of Turkey (about one hundred miles east of the port city of Ephesus) that was first evangelized by one of Paul's converts, is divided into two major sections. In the first section (1:15—3:4), Paul emphasizes all the blessings they have in Christ, and then warns them not to be swayed by the wrong teachings circulating in the community but to keep their eyes firmly fixed on Christ alone—he alone can save them. In the second section (3:5—4:6), much like the second section of Ephesians, he describes the beautiful, Christlike life that they are to live in response to their salvation.

This is the most Christological of Paul's letters, emphasizing that Christ must be the sole focus of a Christian's life and thinking; every part of their life must be grounded in him. Nothing must ever be allowed to take away their trust in Christ alone, for salvation lies solely in him.

5. See p. 8 n. 14.
6. See p. 8 n. 14.

Paul and His Life-Transforming Theology

Outline:

1:1–14	Introduction
1:15—3:4	Christ as the sole focus of a believer's life and trust
3:5—4:6	Exhortation to live as Christians
4:7–18	Final words

1 Thessalonians, one of Paul's earliest letters, written (about AD 50–52) to encourage the new believers who are being persecuted in the key city of northeastern Greece, is divided into two major sections. In the first section (chapters 1–3), Paul gives thanks for God's good work in their lives, reassures them of his own integrity, expresses how concerned he has been for them, and tells them how delighted he is to hear of how well they're doing. In the second section (chapters 4–5), he urges them to live exemplary, sexually moral lives and gives them further instructions—especially on the Second Coming of Christ and the need to be ready for it. With its emphasis on Christ's soon-anticipated return, the letter reminds believers to live as if each day might be their last.

Outline:

1:1–10	Introduction and encouragement
2:1—3:13	Paul's integrity and concern for the believers
4:1—5:24	Exhortation to live as Christians, ready for Christ's return
5:25–28	Final words

2 Thessalonians, written perhaps shortly after 1 Thessalonians (about AD 50–52), addresses two additional problems in the young persecuted church: (1) a rumor that the Day of the Lord has already come and (2) an inclination to laziness on the part of some. This letter reveals Paul's understanding of apocalyptic events associated with the end of the world (though many of the details remain obscure) and his pragmatic approach to practical problems in the church.

Outline:

1:1–12	Introduction
2:1–12	A rumor that Christ has already returned
2:13—3:5	Exhortation to live as Christians

3:6–15	A warning not to be lazy
3:16–18	Final words

1 Timothy, one of the Pastoral Letters (Paul's last letters, written about AD 59–65),[7] is addressed to a trusted assistant who has been posted to Ephesus as Paul's representative to help the young churches in western Turkey. In this letter, Paul gives advice on the organization of the church (including the selection of leaders) and the administration of its programs, and instructs Timothy to stop the wrong teachings that are circulating in the church. He also gives some personal advice to Timothy on his Christian life and his ministry. The letter shows Paul's high standards for Christian leaders; it also shows some of the internal problems the early churches had to deal with, and how Paul responds to them practically. As such, it provides practical advice for those who lead churches today.

Outline:

1:1–2	Introduction
1:3—3:16	Instructions concerning the church and its leaders
4:1—6:21	Paul's advice to Timothy

2 Timothy, also one of the Pastoral Letters, appears to be the last of Paul's letters, written shortly before his execution (about AD 64–65).[8] Imprisoned in Rome, feeling isolated, and knowing that his remaining days are few, Paul urges his younger colleague Timothy to be bold and fearless for Christ and to come see him before he dies. He also gives Timothy additional personal advice and encourages him to keep his personal standards high. The letter shows Paul's courage and confidence in the face of death, and his desire for Timothy to be strong and bold in his witness for Christ and courageous as he carries on the ministry of Paul.

7. See p. 8 n. 15.
8. See p. 8 n. 15.

Paul and His Life-Transforming Theology

Outline:

1:1–2	Introduction
1:3—4:8	Instruction and exhortation to be strong for Christ
4:9–22	Final words

Titus, also one of the Pastoral Letters (written about AD 59–65),9 is addressed to a trusted assistant who has been posted as Paul's representative to the island of Crete to help the young churches there. In this short letter, Paul gives advice on choosing church leaders and emphasizes the importance of believers living a serious, well-disciplined, respectable, godly life. Christians are to be God-fearing people known for doing good, whose lives bear witness to the gospel they proclaim.

Outline:

1:1–4	Introduction
1:5–16	Qualifications for church leadership and the problem of wrong teachings
2:1—3:11	Exhortation of believers to live a godly life, devoted to doing good
3:12–15	Final words

Philemon, written from prison (perhaps about AD 52–55),[10] is addressed to the leader of a home fellowship in Colossae who is a slave-owner. Paul urges him to welcome back Onesimus, a new believer who, as one of Philemon's former slaves, seems to have run away and then been converted through Paul's witness. As a Christian, Philemon is to treat Onesimus no longer merely as a slave but as a brother in Christ. This letter, with its implication that social status means nothing in the family of Christ, eventually played a role in the abolition of slavery. Believers are to relate to one another as caring brothers and sisters, whatever their social standing.

Outline:

1–7	Introduction
8–22	A plea for Onesimus
23–25	Final words

9. See see p. 8 n. 15.
10. See p. 8 n. 14.

Works Cited

Bruce, F. F. *The Letter of Paul to the Romans*. Rev. ed. Tyndale New Testament Commentaries. Grand Rapids: Eerdmans, 1985.

Bunyan, John. *Grace Abounding to the Chief of Sinners*. Edited by Roger Sharrock. Oxford: Clarendon, 1962.

Campbell, Constantine R. *Paul and Union with Christ: An Exegetical and Theological Study*. Grand Rapids: Zondervan, 2012.

Clement. "The Letter of the Romans to the Corinthians (1 Clement)." In *The Apostolic Fathers: Greek Texts and English Translations of Their Writings*, 2nd ed., translated and edited by J. B. Lightfoot and J. R. Farmer, edited and revised by Michael W. Holmes, 23–101. Grand Rapids: Baker, 1992.

Emerson, R. W. "Self-Reliance." In *Essays: 1st Series*. Boston, 1841 / *Essays, Lectures and Orations*. London, 1848: 30.

Eusebius. *The History of the Church from Christ to Constantine*. Translated by G. A. Williamson, revised and edited by Andrew Louth. Penguin Classics. London: Penguin, 1989.

Hemer, Colin J. *The Book of Acts in the Setting of Hellenistic History*. Edited by Conrad H. Gempf. Wissenschaftliche Untersuchungen zum Neuen Testament 49. Tübingen: J. C. B. Mohr, 1989.

Hunter, A. M. *The Gospel According to St Paul*. Philadelphia: Westminster, 1966.

Hurtado, L. W. "Lord." In *Dictionary of Paul and His Letters*, 560–69. Downers Grove, IL: InterVarsity, 1993.

Jerome. *De Virii Illistribus* (Lives of Illustrious Men). In *Nicene and Post-Nicene Fathers: Second Series*, vol. 3, translated by Ernest Cushing Richardson, edited by Philip Schaff and Henry Wace, 359–84. Peabody, MA: Hendrickson, 2004.

Kelly, J. N. D. *The Pastoral Epistles*. Black's New Testament Commentaries. Peabody, MA: Hendrickson, 2009.

Luther, Martin. *Commentary on the Epistle to the Romans*. Translated by J. Theodore Mueller. Grand Rapids: Zondervan, 1954.

———. *Luther's Works* 54. Translated and edited by Theodore G. Tappert. Philadelphia: Fortress, 1967.

McGrath, Alister E., editor. *The Christian Theology Reader*. 2nd ed. Oxford: Blackwell, 2001.

Mohrlang, Roger. "Love." In *Dictionary of Paul and His Letters*, 575–78. Downers Grove, IL: InterVarsity, 1993.

————. *Matthew and Paul: A Comparison of Ethical Perspectives*. Society for New Testament Studies Monograph Series 48. Cambridge: Cambridge University Press, 1984, 2005.

————. "Paul." In *Jesus in History, Thought, and Culture: An Encyclopedia*, edited by Leslie Houlden, 679–88. Oxford: ABC-CLIO, 2003. Also in paperback edition, *Jesus: The Complete Guide*. New York: Continuum, 2006.

————. "Romans." In *Romans, Galatians: Cornerstone Biblical Commentary*, vol. 14, 1–244. Carol Stream, IL: Tyndale House, 2007.

Stupperich, R. "Luther." In *Eerdmans' Handbook to the History of Christianity*, edited by Tim Dowley, 362–66. Berkhamsted, UK: Lion, 1977.

Thistleton, Anthony C. *The Living Paul: An Introduction to the Apostle's Life and Thought*. Downers Grove, IL: InterVarsity, 2009.

Thrall, Margaret. *The Second Epistle to the Corinthians*. 2 vols. International Critical Commentary. New York: T. & T. Clark , vol. 1 1994/2004, vol. 2 2000/2004.

Tozer, A. W. *The Knowledge of the Holy*. San Francisco: HarperSanFrancisco, 1978.

Wenham, David. *Paul: Follower of Jesus or Founder of Christianity?* Grand Rapids: Eerdmans, 1995.

Wikipedia, s.v. "Christian eschatology," http://en.wikipedia.org/wiki/Christian_eschatology (accessed January 20, 2013).

Wright, N. T. *Paul in Fresh Perspective*. Minneapolis: Fortress, 2005.